From
Margin to Center

The MIT Press Cambridge, Massachusetts London, England

Julie H. Reiss

From
Margin to Center

The Spaces of Installation Art

This book was set in Bembo by Mary Reilly and was printed and bound in the United States of America.

Library of Congress Cataloging-in-Publication Data

Reiss, Julie H.

    From margin to center : the spaces of installation art / Julie H. Reiss.

       p. m.

    Includes bibliographical references and index.

    ISBN 0-262-18196-7 (alk. paper)

    1. Installations (Art)—New York (State)—New York.

  2.   Installations (Art) I. Title

N65735.N5R45 2000

709´.04' 074—dc21   99-41769

                                    CIP

To Tim, Sophia, and Matthew, in celebration of the life we share.

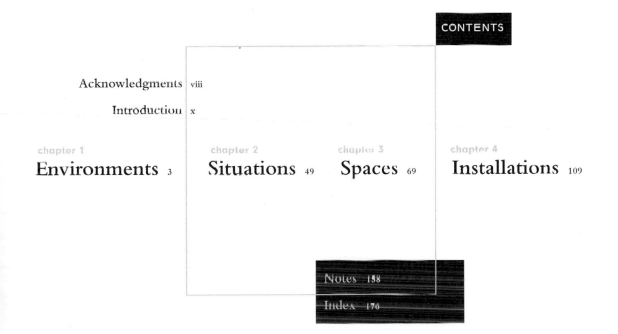

CONTENTS

Acknowledgments

I am deeply grateful to Jim Dine, Patrick Ireland, Ilya Kabakov, Allan Kaprow, Charlotta Kotik, Jennifer Winkworth, Claes Oldenburg, and Robert Storr for the interviews they granted me early on. I gratefully acknowledge Jack Flam for his sustained interest in this project, for guiding me through the process of publishing a book. Roger Conover at The MIT Press was encouraging and forthright from our first contact. The students in my Installation art seminar at Purchase College helped me to see the need for this book, and to set the parameters for it.

I am extremely fortunate in the support I have from family and friends. In particular, my mother, Johanna Reiss, and my sister, Kathy Reiss, are the foundation that has given me the courage to pursue my interests. Valerie Marcus and I have shared in each other's lives for over two decades. I have benefited greatly, in both tangible and intangible ways, from the involvement in my life of my aunt, Lucy Foster (1926–99), and my uncle, Michael Foster. Louise Kirkpatrick, Mrs. Robert L. Kirkpatrick, and Bob and Joyce Kirkpatrick have bolstered me with their encouragement. I have more than once called on Lisa Panzesa for her perspective. My husband, Tim Forker, has contributed to this book in myriad ways. I have relied on his enduring patience, his sense of humor, his editorial skills, and his love.

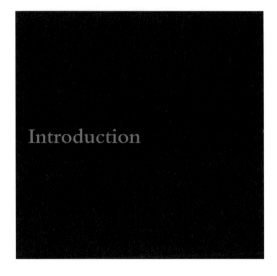

Introduction

This book seeks to fill a void in the study of art since 1960: namely, the study of Installation art. The term "Installation art" is a relatively new one, emerging years after many of the works to which it can be applied were created. Although its definition is somewhat elusive, the term can be used to describe works that share certain key characteristics. In viewing such works, it is important to separate them from other modes of artistic practice, allowing that which is unique about them to be illuminated, and helping the works to be better understood.

Before the term "Installation art" became part of the vernacular of contemporary art, there was the term "Environment," which was used by Allan Kaprow in 1958 to describe his room-size multimedia works.[1] This term was picked up by critics and used to describe a range of works for two decades. In the mid–1970s, the term "Environment," while still popular, was joined by others, including "project art" and simply "temporary art." Eventually there was a shift in terminology. But it was not from Environment to Installation art but, rather, from exhibition to installation. The artist Daniel Buren recognized this in 1971 in his essay "The Function of the Studio." Writing about the need to preserve the relationship between the work and its place of production, he asked: "Hasn't the term *installation* come to replace *exhibition*?"[2] Installation began to be used interchangeably with exhibition to describe work produced at the exhibition site. All Environments (according to Kaprow's conception of the term) could also be described as installations, but the reverse is not true. The shift from the term "Environment" to the term "installation" was a gradual one, and even the recognition of an artistic practice called Environments was slow to become established. Despite the prevalence of the word "Environment" in exhibition reviews beginning in 1959, it did not appear in *The Art Index* until volume 18, November 1969 to October 1970. There, for the first time, "Environment (Art)" appeared. The first issue of *The Art Index* that lists installations is volume 27, November 1978 to October 1979. Under "Installation," the researcher is advised to "see Environment (Art)." In the next fourteen volumes, "installation" continues to be indexed with no listings other than a cross-reference to Environment. Not until volume 42, November 1993 to October 1994 does "installation" appear with an actual listing of articles. At that point, Environment ceases to be a category.

The term "installation" appeared as its own listing in general reference books sooner than it did in *The Art Index*. *The Oxford Dictionary of Art* (1988) defines installation as a "term which came into vogue during the 1970s for an assemblage or environment constructed in the gallery specifically for a particular exhibition."[3] The *Glossary of Art, Architecture and Design Since 1945* (1992) concurs: "the word 'installation' has taken on a stronger meaning, i.e., a one-off exhibit fabricated in relation to the specific characteristics of a gallery space. . . . In the late 1980s some artists began to specialize in constructing installations with the result that a specific genre— 'Installation Art'—came into being."[4] "Environment" can still be found in recent reference books. Edward Lucie-Smith in *The Thames and Hudson Dictionary of Art Terms* (1984) defines Environment as a "term used from the late 1950s for a three-dimensional work of art, often of a temporary nature, which the viewer can enter (although in practice exhibiting authorities often prevent this)."[5]

Installation art can be abstract or pictorial, controlled or spontaneous. Separate objects can be included, or no objects at all. There is always a reciprocal relationship of some kind between the viewer and the work, the work and the space, and the space and the viewer. One could argue that these qualities define many artistic practices. To refine the definition further, therefore, one might add that in creating an installation, the artist treats an entire indoor space (large enough for people to enter) as a single situation, rather than as a gallery for displaying separate works. The spectator is in some way regarded as integral to the completion of the work Although the term "Installation art" has become widely used, it is still relatively nonspecific. It refers to a wide range of artistic practices, and at times overlaps with other interrelated areas including Fluxus, Earth art, Minimalism, video art, Performance art, Conceptual art and Process art. Site specificity, institutional critique, temporality, and ephemerality are issues shared by many practitioners of these genres. While establishing the autonomy of Installation art, we must also examine its relationship to other forms.

The essence of Installation art is spectator participation, but the definition of participation varies greatly from one artist to another, and even from one work to another by the same artist. Participation can mean offering the viewer specific activities It can also mean demanding that the viewer walk through the space and simply confront what is there. Objects may fall directly in the viewer's path or become evident only through exploration of a space. In each of these situations, the viewer is required to complete the piece; the meaning evolves from the interaction between the two. Art that acknowledges the presence of the viewer was condemned as "theatrical" by Michael Fried in his 1967 essay, "Art and Objecthood." [6] He saw theatricality as the rift between Minimalism and modernism, and, by extension, between modernism and any art that includes the spectator. Although specifically aimed at Minimalism, Fried's critique set down several factors that illuminate Installation art in a broad sense: the temporal nature of the art, its dependence upon a particular situation, and its focus on the beholder.

Spectator participation is so integral to Installation art that without having the experience of being in the piece, analysis of Installation art is difficult. Perhaps as a result, few historians have seriously studied it despite its proliferation as an art form in the last forty years. As recently as 1993, Arthur Danto wrote of Installation art that "it is impossible to speak of any one piece without having undergone the experience it demands." Therefore, at the time of the catalog's publication, he did not even attempt to discuss the works yet to be installed in *From the Inside Out: Eight Contemporary Artists,* an exhibition of Installation art at the Jewish Museum in New York.[7]

My intent is not to create a complete survey of all installation-type activity over the past four decades. Given the scant literature devoted to Installation art, it is more fruitful to focus on some of the central figures in the emergence of the genre.[8] These include not only the artists who create the works, but the individuals—including artists, critics, and curators—who discuss them. Primary focus will be given to installations created in New York City beginning in the late 1950s. There were important related activities happening elsewhere in the United States and abroad, but the complex and rich history of Installation art that is intertwined with the particulars of exhibition spaces and the artistic community of New York provides ample justification for a geographical limit.

Another focal point of this book is the gradual assimilation of Installation art into mainstream museums and galleries. Originally presented primarily in alternative art spaces, installations have been routinely commissioned by major art museums and galleries since the early 1990s. The move of Installation art from the margin of the art world to its center has had far-reaching effects on the works created and on museum practice. In a broader sense, Installation art can be used as a barometer for the historical relationship between avant-garde art and the museum

Installation art has been an important development in the twentieth century, but it has received only marginal scholarly attention. Because Installation art is not easily collected and thus not easily experienced after it is dismantled, it has resisted traditional art historical approaches. Indeed this resistance to historicization has been the lure for many of the artists who have chosen to work in this genre. There are other modes of artistic practice even more transient—artists' fleeting gestures or acts that cannot be collected or stored except in memory An example would be Vito Acconci's *Following Piece*, done in New York in 1969. Acconci would choose people on the street at random and, unbeknownst to them, follow them until they went off the street into a private domain such as a home or office. Installation art, however, has a physical presence while it is on view, and this allows for it to be reconstructed in a sense, using several different methods.

There are four main sources for dismantled Installation art that can be used by the historian. One is the published criticism of the works. Reviewers see the works, walk through them, spend time in them and based on this, they describe them. Their reviews not only demonstrate what was considered important about this revolutionary art form at any given time, they function as eyewitness reports. That it is the report of only one individual does not diminish its importance, as first-person experience is one of the main points of Installation art.

Individuals whose work has been important in the development of Installation art can be interviewed, including artists, curators and critics. Their memories, perspectives, and published writings form a second valuable source of information.

Another major source for historians is photography of the installations, whether it be for a museum catalog or an informal shot made in an alternative space. Photographs of objects have assumed an enormously significant role in the study of art. In 1953 André Malraux observed that "for the last hundred years . . . art history has been the history of that which can be photographed."[9] He is referring to the use of photography as reproduction rather than documentation, but for Installation art, documentation is all that is possible. Without photographic documentation, Installation art would likely be even more peripheral to art history than it already is. The photograph preserves ephemeral art, and many major installations have been photographed. Because it is documentation rather than reproduction (a two-dimensional image of a three-dimensional space), the photograph of an installation cannot function as a substitute for the original. Although one can glean a certain amount of visual information from a photograph of an installation, one must avoid the temptation to use the photograph as if it were a reproduction and to formally analyze the piece based on it alone. Still, the photograph can be an extremely useful tool if viewed critically. The way an installation has been photographed says a great deal about the piece and its context. I recall an incident during my tenure at the Jewish Museum in New York. Ilya Kabakov was perturbed that the museum staff had his installation, *Mother and Son,* photographed without spectators for an exhibition catalog (figure I.1). His feeling was that spectators were integral to the piece and should have been included. But this had never occurred to the museum staff. Their main concern was to find an architectural photographer who would be able to successfully photograph a whole space as opposed to a discrete object.

The fourth way to approach Installation art is through the context in which it was exhibited. Installation art is and always has been a public art form. (The great historical exception may be Kurt Schwitters's three *Merzbau.* The first and most elaborate one, which

I.1
Ilya Kabakov, *Mother and Son,* 1993. Mixed media installation. Installation view of *From the Inside Out: Eight Contemporary Artists.* Jewish Museum, New York. 13 June 1993 through 14 January 1994. Photograph © Patricia Layman Bazelon. Courtesy Barbara Gladstone Gallery.

I.2
Kurt Schwitters,
Merzbau, 1933.
Photograph
courtesy Sprengel
Museum Hannover.

developed out of a column the artist had begun in 1919, was done in Schwitters's own home in Hannover, Germany[10] [figure I.2]. The other two versions, begun in 1937 and 1947, respectively, were also done on private, although not residential, premises.) Historically, Installation art has been a showcase form, due in part to its site-specific nature. Although not unheard of, it is atypical for an installation to be fully created in the privacy of an artist's studio and then be dismantled and transferred to a more public place. Installation art is usually dependent on the configurations of a particular space or situation. Even if the same installation is remade in more than one location, it will not be exactly the same in two places, owing to the differences between spaces. The physical characteristics of the space have an enormous effect on the final product.

The past four decades have witnessed a surge of interest from both artists and critics alike in the effect of exhibition context on a work of art. The notion of a "neutral" exhibition space has gradually been eroded. The history of exhibition locale is inextricably intertwined with the history of Installation art on several levels. Physical properties of the spaces—the raw, unfinished "alternative" space, or a pristine white gallery—are enormously important in installations where the space becomes integrated into the work. Through its decrepitude, a raw space can represent continuity between the installation and the street. Or a break between the installation and the world outside can be communicated through the rarefied atmosphere of a museum. Moreover, the status of the spaces vis-à-vis the art world has an effect on the status of the works shown. Institutional context has the power to validate works or relegate them to the margin. The spaces are an important part of Installation art's history.

The starting point for a history of Installation art is open to question; there is no consensus at present. Deciding where Installation art began depends on who is presenting the history and for what purpose. In 1958 Kaprow proposed that Environments evolved from 1950s American action painting (particularly that of Jackson Pollock), and from late 1950s assemblage.[11] In 1969, however, Jennifer Licht, writing the catalog essay for *Spaces*—the first exhibition of Installation art at the Museum of Modern Art—cited Schwitters as the most direct prototype for Kaprow and his contemporaries.[12] She thus placed their work solidly in a European framework, reflecting the museum's general bias.

In addition to Kaprow's suggested lineage, there was other important environmental painting and sculpture done in New York in the 1950s and early 1960s that should be taken into account in constructing a history of Installation art. Frederick Kiesler exhibited his *Galaxies* at the Sidney Janis Gallery in 1954, extending thematically related units of painting into the entire space, including the floor and ceiling. The largest of these groupings, *Horse Galaxy,* showed views of a horse from different angles. The viewer was surrounded by the work in every direction (figure I.3).[13] Beginning in 1955, Louise Nevelson created Environments that comprised individual sculptures that could later be reassembled in different arrangements or incorporated into other Environments. One of the most dramatic examples of these installations was *Moon Garden + One,* exhibited in 1958 at the Grand Central Moderns Gallery. Nevelson created an all-black Environment with walls of stacked boxes and free-standing sculptures. Richard Marshall said of Nevelson's Environments that "these thematic installations were planned to be environmental in the architectural sense and designed so that the sculptures physically surrounded the viewer and often made use of all available space."[14]

Herbert Ferber exhibited a full-scale environmental sculpture at the Whitney Museum in 1961. Commissioned by the museum, *Sculpture as Environment* filled a gallery in the Whitney's West 54th Street location with twisting papier-mâché forms protruding from the walls, ceiling, and floor (figure I.4). "One had to literally explore the work of art," recalled George Dennison.[15] These examples by established

I.3
Frederick Kiesler, *Galaxies.* Installation view at the Sidney Janis Gallery, New York, 1954. Photograph by Geoffrey Clements.

artists in other media may have helped pave the way for later developments.

A broad attempt to historicize Installation art was made by Germano Celant for the 1976 Venice Biennale. The guiding principle for this international survey, entitled *Ambiente Arte,* was artists who worked on a room-size scale. Celant provided a historical section as well as a contemporary one. The exhibition began with the Italian Futurists, Russian Constructivists, and Dutch de Stijl artists. Celant included Pollock, Kaprow, and Nevelson in one of the later sections.[16]

European precedents are undoubtedly important to Installation

I.4
Installation view of the exhibition *A Sculpture by Herbert Ferber to Create an Environment.* Papier-mâché, 12 x 24 feet, diameter 15 feet. Whitney Museum of American Art, 10 March through 23 April 1961. Photograph by Eric Pollitzer. Courtesy Jim Strong.

European precedents are undoubtedly important to Installation art's overall history. El Lissitzky's *Proun Room* (constructed for the Grosse Berliner Ausstellung at the Landesausstellungsgebäude in Berlin in 1923), the painted abstract environments of de Stijl artists, and Schwitters's *Merzbau* are all important precedents in part because they were made by artists who figure among the most important pioneers of modernism. In a sense, these works gave permission to later artists to create room-size works of art, which the viewer could enter. The early works paved the way to a variety of possibilities, and at times may well have served as models in the abstract for later artists. For example, Schwitters's Hannover *Merzbau* had cut through its original domestic interior, and in later stages reached the exterior. In New York in 1970, George Trakas made ↑↓ *(The Piece That Went Through the Floor)* and ⇆ *(The Piece That Went Through the Window)*, two site-specific installations that contained a similar relationship to interior and exterior space (figure I.5). Moreover, the early European examples were generally not done for conventional art museums. They were often done in temporary exhibition halls or in galleries.[17] In this way they presage the status of Installation art in New York in the 1950s, 1960s, and 1970s.

European precedents can also be found for the discussion of spectator participation, an issue that was addressed early in the twentieth century by Lissitzky, giving one starting point to this discourse. Lissitzky wanted to make the experience of his art active for the viewer. Regarding *Proun Room*, he stated that "one keeps on moving round in an exhibition. Therefore the room should be so organized that of itself it provides an inducement to walk around it."[18] Lissitzky's interest in the viewer's experience carried through to those exhibitions in which he designed the space for other artists' work. In the *Raum für konstruktive Kunst* (Room for constructivist art) that he designed in Dresden for the Internationale Ausstellung in 1926, shifting panels allowed the spectators to control their experience of viewing the art on the walls.[19] At the time, Lissitzky said that "if on previous occasions in his march-past in front of the picture-walls, he was lulled by the painting into a certain *passivity,* now our design should make the man *active*. This should be the purpose of the room."[20] Lissitzky's sentiments were prophetic. The desire to shake the spectator out of a passive, spongelike state and instead have a self-determined, active experience is borne out in the chapters to follow.

I.5
George Trakas, *(The Piece That Went Through the Window)*, 112 Greene Street, New York, September 1970. Wood, wire, tempered glass, sawdust, 56 x 201 x 64 inches. Photograph by Richard Landry.

From
Margin to **Center**

CHAPTER 1

Environments

"From September 11 through September 22—from eleven in the morning to eleven at night—people coming to the Smolin Gallery at 19 East 71 St. singly, in pairs, or in groups, for the fifty cent admission, will have the thrill of active participation in an Environment created by Allan Kaprow."[1] So read the press release for Allan Kaprow's 1962 Environment, *Words*, perhaps the closest thing to a free-for-all that New York gallery goers had ever experienced. Visitors to the exhibition (or participants, as they were referred to by the artist) could write words on papers provided for this purpose and add them to the words that already covered the walls of the first of the two rooms of *Words*. Words on rollers allowed the participant to change the words that were visible at any one time. Chalk, crayon, and pencil were provided in the second room, to facilitate the addition of messages, words, or phrases there (figure 1.1).

Words was the most elaborate Environment Kaprow had created thus far. He had exhibited his first Environment four years earlier, at the Hansa Gallery, an artist-run cooperative in New York, and had followed up with several more before *Words*. Although his were not the first room-size, environmental works shown in the city, they nonetheless provide a starting point for a history of this genre in New York. Kaprow's Environments received a fair amount of critical attention, given that he was a relatively unknown young artist. Kaprow provided his own definition of an Environment along with the work, and his definition seemed to catch on. Kaprow wrote and published articles, which contributed to his being regarded as a leader of a new "movement" by some critics because it gave him a platform for his ideas and thus greater visibility. The other artists associated with Kaprow at this time included Jim Dine, Claes Oldenburg, and Robert

1.1
Allan Kaprow,
Words, 1962.
Rearrangeable
Environment with
lights and sounds.
Smolin Gallery,
New York, 1962.
Photograph by
Robert R. McElroy.

Whitman, by virtue of their construction of Environments, their shared interest in performances or Happenings, and their association with each other.

These artists knew each other, and to some extent worked together, but from the outset they were each following their individual paths. Admittedly, it was sometimes convenient to be a group, as Dine recalls: "We were asked to be members of this clique and jumped at it . . . because it was nice to be included, it was nice to say Kaprow, Oldenburg and Dine, Whitman. . . . But in the end, I don't think one person had anything to do with the other person."[2] Historical distance allows for the sorting through of individual endeavors, and also for connections. Claes Oldenburg acknowledged Kaprow's breakthroughs even though he did not like the term "Happening" being applied to his performances and disliked the term "Environment," because these were Kaprow's words.[3] But in an interview for *Artforum* in February 1966, Oldenburg conceded respect for Kaprow: "The only reason I have taken up Happenings is because I wanted to experiment with total space or surrounding space. I don't believe that anyone has ever used space before in the way Kaprow and others have been using it in Happenings. There are many ways to interpret a Happening, but one way is to use it as an extension of painting space."[4]

Kurt Schwitters's *Merzbau*, the Futurist theories on the interpenetration of objects and space, and Duchamp's mile of string at the *First Papers of Surrealism* exhibition in New York in 1942 (figure 1.2.) are often cited by art historians as precedents for the Environments of Allan Kaprow and his contemporaries.[5] Dada theories were disseminated in the 1950s largely through Robert Motherwell's book, *The*

Dada Painters and Poets, which had been published in 1951 and was widely circulated.

Kaprow acknowledges the impact of *The Dada Painters and Poets*—especially the Dada theories—on his own development. There are no illustrations included in the book of Schwitters's *Merzbau,* but there is an essay by Schwitters that talks about his drive toward the creation of a total work of art—something that was to intrigue Kaprow as well. Kaprow also read literature on Italian Futurism and Russian Constructivism and, as he has stated: "I began to discover in a minor way . . . that what I was interested in doing had plenty of prototypes in art history."[6] Ultimately, however, Kaprow suggested a different line of development for Environments, one which looked toward more immediate American sources.

1.2
Marcel Duchamp,
One Mile of String.
Installation of the
exhibition *First
Papers of Surrealism.*
New York,
14 October through
17 November 1942.
Photograph by
John Schiff.
Courtesy
Philadelphia
Museum of Art.

Kaprow wrote "The Legacy of Jackson Pollock" in 1956, and it was published in *Art News* two years later. In this article, he put forth the notion that the arena created by American action painting led artists first to assemblages and ultimately to three-dimensional spaces, or Environments. This progression from painting to assemblage to Environment described Kaprow's own artistic development as well as that of Jim Dine.[7] Oldenburg, however, came to Environments through sculpture.

Although Kaprow saw Environments and Happenings as interrelated, it is the Environments that introduce many issues germane to Installation art. In 1966, after several years of planning, Kaprow published the book *Assemblage, Environments and Happenings.* The ideas in the book had already been partially disseminated five years earlier when William Seitz quoted from the then unpublished manuscript in the catalog to the exhibition at the Museum of Modern Art, *The Art of Assemblage.*[8] In quoting from the manuscript, Seitz accepts Kaprow's theory that Environments and Happenings developed out of assemblage. In addition to the importance of the text, Kaprow's book remains a valuable source of images of works no longer extant. There are some pointed juxtapositions. For example, Kaprow places a photograph of himself in his Environment *Yard* opposite a photograph of Jackson Pollock at work in his studio.

In order to avoid too much overlap with Michael Kirby's book, *Happenings,* which had been released the previous year, Kaprow chose a different selection of artists to include in the Happenings section of his book.[9] Unlike Kirby, few of the artists he chose were American. He included Wolf Vostell, the Gutai Group, Milan Knizak, Jean-

Jacques Lebel, George Brecht, and Kenneth Dewey, but in the section of the book devoted to Environments, he included works by Oldenburg and Dine. In addition to providing photographs of assemblages, Environments, and Happenings, he elaborated on the progression, saying that assemblages and Environments "are at root the same—the only difference is one of size. Assemblages may be handled or walked around, while Environments must be walked into. Though scale obviously makes all the experiential difference in the world, a similar form principle controls each of these approaches, and some artists work in both with great ease."[10]

Kaprow's Environments focused on the idea of active spectator participation. This was of paramount importance to Kaprow in a way that it was not to other artists with whom he was associated. Although he exhibited with Robert Whitman, Claes Oldenburg, and Jim Dine, among others, he has said that he feels his true affinities were with Wolf Vostell, Milan Knizak, and Jean-Jacques Lebel, who, in their performances, were greatly interested in involving the audience. But as Kaprow has also said, "the press noise misled everybody into thinking [audience participation] was a massive movement."[11] Kaprow's Environments were conceived with active and fairly specific participation of the spectator in mind; this involvement was part of the whole spirit of the works, and consistent with Kaprow's philosophy of integrating art and life.

The importance to Kaprow of spectator participation in Environments is borne out by his eventual development of Happenings, which, in Kaprow's case, ultimately eliminated the audience altogether, leaving only participants. The progression, as he would later describe it, was fairly rapid:

There was a sense of mystery [in the Environments] until your eye reached a wall. Then there was a dead end. . . . I tried camouflaging the walls one way or another. I tried destroying the sense of bounded space with more sound than ever, played continuously. Hidden up in the lights were all kinds of toys that I had gimmicked up so that it was impossible to tell their identity: bells, tinkles, rattles, grinders, marbles in tin cans that turned over, and so on. But this was no solution. It only increased the growing discord between my work and the art gallery's space and connotations. I immediately saw that every visitor to the Environment was part of it. I had not really thought of it before. And so I gave him occupations like moving something, turning switches on—just a few things. Increasingly during 1957 and 1958, this suggested a more "scored" responsibility for that visitor. I offered him more and more to do, until there developed the Happening.[12]

The notion of involving the audience, whether in an assemblage, Environment, or Happening (and Kaprow offered active involvement in all three), also came to him in part out of the teachings of John Cage, with whom he had studied at the New School for Social Research. Cage had taught a class there called "Composition as Experimental Music," and it was in this class, in 1957, that Kaprow staged his first Happening. Regarding the Happenings, Kaprow has said, "a lot of these things were actually set up very much under the permissions granted by John Cage."[13]

For Kaprow, spectator participation in an Environment meant there was some specific activity for the viewer. Kaprow's assemblages in the late 1950s had already begun to offer some activity, although they were still freestanding, discrete objects, and could not be entered. *Penny Arcade,* an assemblage presented at the Hansa Gallery in 1956, had canvas strips hung in front of works that the viewer had to move aside or peer through in order to see the works hung on the wall. *Wall*, 1957–59, had rearrangeable panels for the viewers to manipulate. The activity in some of the Environments had to do with the demands on the viewer in traversing the piece. *An Apple Shrine*, presented at the Judson Gallery in 1960, was a mazelike labyrinth with newspaper on the floor, through which viewers shuffled as they walked. The narrow alleyways and the newspapers forced the viewers to physically interact with the pieces and, one imagines, with each other (figure 1.3). *Yard,* presented in the courtyard of the Martha Jackson Gallery in 1961, required the viewer to walk on piles of tires (figure 1.4).

Words was presented in 1962 at the Smolin Gallery and again in 1963 at the State University of New York at Stony Brook. In both versions, *Words* consisted of two rooms separated by muslin curtains. Rose Moose's description in the catalog that accompanied the 1962 presentation describes how there were signs directing the viewer to "turn on the phonographs; roll the rollers; add your own words."[14] *Words* provided the opportunity for the spectator to participate, but it was also controlled to a certain degree. Not only had Kaprow established separate activities appropriate to each of the two rooms, but there was a particular direction the viewer had to take, a path to follow. As Kaprow stated in the catalog:

Of course, being active, we can misuse any environment, natural or artistic. We can destroy a landscape through carelessness, and here we can refuse to consider what responses are appropriate to the nature of the idea. For instance, it is inappropriate to staple word-strips askew, onto the floor or any-

1.4
Allan Kaprow, *Yard*, 1961. Installation view of the exhibition *Environments, Situations, Spaces*. Martha Jackson Gallery, New York, 1961. Photograph by Robert R. McElroy.

where in the smaller room; and it would be just as unfit to write with the colored chalks in the larger room. There are freedoms for the visitor (as there are for the artist), but they are revealed only within the limits dictated by the art work's immediate as well as underlying themes.[15]

Kaprow offered a reciprocal relationship between the work and the viewer. Something could be contributed by the spectator within the structure established by the artist. The words added by one viewer would become part of the piece, available to the next viewer to read. The visitors helped to create the work, to complete it. The situation provided an active experience for the viewer.

Kaprow's accompanying statement in the catalog for *Words* in 1962 shows that his intention with the Environment was to break down barriers between the spectator and the work of art:

Words is an "environment," the name given to an art that one enters, submits to, and is—in turn—influenced by. If it is different from most art in its impermanence and changeableness, it is like much contemporary work in being fashioned from the real and everyday world. . . . I am involved with the city atmosphere of billboards, newspapers, scrawled pavements and alley walls, in the drone of a lecture, whispered secrets, pitchmen in Times Square fun-parlors, bits of stories and conversations overheard at the Automat. All this has been compressed and shaped into a situation which, in order to "live" in the fullest sense, must actively engage a visitor. This may be difficult for those bound by the habits of respectful distance essential for older art. But if we temporarily put aside the question of the sacred in aesthetic matters and see in Words activities analogous to some in which we normally engage—doodling, playing anagrams or Scrabble, searching for just the right word to express a thought, climbing a ladder to hang a picture on the wall, listening to records, leaving notes for someone—then the accessibility of the work may get across and its art as much as its mystery becomes apparent. I doubt that mere passive observation is very rewarding.[16]

In his drive to shift the viewer from a passive state to an active one, Kaprow was reflecting a wider cultural shift that would increase throughout the 1960s. Passivity was becoming regarded as a negative virtue, even a threat to democracy. Andrew Ross refers to the "'cultural crusade' to replace 'passivity' with 'participation'" that was expressed in the work of Marshall McLuhan, for example, later in the decade.[17] Kaprow himself would later specifically relate his work to the ideals of the time:

Do you remember the popularization of some of the ingredients of Happenings in those things called be-ins and do-ins? It was a kind of communitarian notion of . . . participation. Everyone would get together a lot more successfully than in Environments and Happenings and . . . they'd form magic circles and sing and chant . . . and I think something of that spirit of participation in a very rudimentary and simple but nevertheless moving way was where the philosophy of Environments and Happenings really emerged—not in the artists' work but in the public sector, and it did in a way that some artists might find uninteresting.[18]

Although Kaprow acknowledges that there was an explicit element of democratic ideals in his Environments and Happenings, it was not as explicit in the works of his American contemporaries. This is interesting because, as Kaprow said, "I would say that the notion of interaction was isolated [in the U.S.] and easy to get into as a philosophy of democracy for the Europeans, strangely enough. It should have been here, but it wasn't."[19]

There was no explicit political content in the Environments of Kaprow, Oldenburg, and Dine. Kaprow vividly recalls that the post-McCarthy era was one in which many artists were afraid to make any explicit political statements. At Rutgers University, where Kaprow taught art history, and where several faculty members had been dismissed during the McCarthy era, Kaprow had been told that he was expected to make no waves.[20] The political implications of Kaprow's Environments were subtle. They hinged on his use of spectator participation, which was consistent with the notion of participatory democracy. This idea existed in spirit years before it was named in the Port Huron statement of 1962. It has applications for the artistic community as well as for the countercultural movements spawned by the civil rights movement. Works involving direct involvement for the visitor, produced at cooperative or community-run exhibition spaces, must be understood in this context.[21]

In discussing the notion of participation in the Environments by Kaprow, Oldenburg, and Dine, one must be careful to separate the critical rhetoric from the reality of the artists' intentions. The critical response to Environments, which depended almost solely on Kaprow, put a misleading emphasis on spectator participation in Environments, giving the impression that it was a primary goal for all concerned. For example, in a group show in which all three artists participated, one reviewer announced: "The young avant-gardes now showing at the Martha Jackson and adjoining David Andersen galleries in New York . . . intend to make every viewer an active, functioning participant in their weird and unsettling art."[22] Kaprow, a self-described "word monger" at the time, is partly responsible for the stamping of other artists with his particular mode.[23] Spectator participation was part of the agenda for Oldenburg and Dine in the years that they were creating Environments, but in a different way and to a far less explicit degree than for Kaprow. In 1960, when Dine and Oldenburg constructed Environments at the Judson Gallery (under the collective name of Ray-Gun,) part of the exhibition was to allow visitors in the gallery to see the works under construction "in order to encourage participation," as stated by the artists in the Spring calendar of events at the Judson Gallery.[24] In a conversation with Barbara Haskell in 1984, Oldenburg said that his Environment, *The Street*, did include an aspect of spectator participation. As Haskell relates, "Oldenburg invited the audience to add its own debris to the floor of *The Street* and encouraged other artists to pin up anything whatsoever on the 'communication board' he had set up adjacent to the gallery."[25] But this was quite different from the activities which Kaprow was offering spectators at the time. Dine never included any activities for the viewer in his Environments. He said later: "For me, frankly, what I did in so-called Environments was just larger works than painting or sculpture could be at that time. . . . I never wanted anyone to be part of my art other than to take from it, you know, take part, but I don't want anyone to participate."[26] Despite the fact that Oldenburg and Dine were not interested in spectator participation in the way that Allan Kaprow was, this was the aspect of their Environments that struck a nerve with the critics.

It is probable that spectator participation has also become so strongly attached to the overall discussion of Environments because of the overlap between Environments and Happenings. Kaprow's Happenings eventually ceased to involve an audience at all; everyone present was a participant. Moreover, many Environments were constructed and exhibited without related Happenings, and Happenings sometimes took place in traditional theater settings with the audience facing the action and not entering the space. Sometimes the audience could only peer through the door, as was the case with Oldenburg's performance of *Snapshots of the City* at the Judson Gallery in 1960. When Happenings were staged in Environments, there was not always a direct connection between the two. At times, it was a marriage of convenience, as with Jim Dine's Environment *The House*, which was shown at the Judson Gallery early in 1960. *The House* became the setting for his performance *The Smiling Workman,* simply because it was available space; the performance was not related conceptually to the Environment.[27] Oldenburg's Environment *The Street,* shown at Judson at the same time, was the setting for his *Snapshots of the City,* but there was more of a conceptual overlap because the performances consisted of encounters such as one might have on city streets. Still, the performance and the Environment were initially conceived by the artist as two separate entities. As Oldenburg later related:

The original performance was supposed to take place in front of the Judson on Thompson Street. It was called *Post No Bills.* We had planned to block the street at the moment of performance by stalling a car, but the more I thought about the piece, the more I felt it was very closely connected with the construction I had made. I decided that I wanted to show my construction at the same time that I presented a performance. . . . So, from my first performance, my theatre work was linked to my sculpture or construction.[28]

Later in 1960, Oldenburg remade *The Street* for an exhibition at the Reuben Gallery. He cleaned up the piece considerably, eliminating much of the debris that had been in the original version, and exhibited it without any performance at all. In his journal he referred to the Reuben Gallery version as the "environmental counterpart" of the Judson work.[29] It could stand alone as an art exhibit, and clearly was not merely the scenery for a performance that had occurred. In November of 1960, Dine staged the Happening *Car Crash,* at the Reuben Gallery. Everything in the performance space was painted white, including all the props, which were chosen to evoke a hospital or emergency room situation. Although designed specifically to relate to the performance, Dine said in retrospect that "the set [for *Car Crash*] was as strong an environment as I ever built, without the people"[30] (figure 1.5).

Claes Oldenburg's *The Store,* which ran from 1 December 1961 through 31 January 1962 at 107 East Second Street, is a good example of the overlap between Environment and performance (figure 1.6). Oldenburg was present whenever *The Store* was open, selling the individual pieces that made up the Environment. It was essentially a performance the Environment provided the setting of an actual store (or technically a gallery, because art was the merchandise). Oldenburg functioned as the proprietor as well as the manufacturer, because the store contained his studio, where the merchandise was created. The artist has cited prototypes for *The Store* in Chicago, where some artists used stores, rather than lofts, as studios.[31]

In Oldenburg's *The Store,* the viewer was synonymous with the customer and could participate, in the fashion of customers everywhere, by browsing and perhaps purchasing. These activities contributed to erasing the boundaries between art and life. *The Store* was sponsored by the Green Gallery, and Oldenburg recalls that most people who came to see it knew what it was about ahead of time. People in the neighborhood did not just come in off the street.[32] After *The Store* closed, Oldenburg staged a series of performances in the back of the space under the collective title of the Ray-Gun Manufacturing Company. To attend the performance, visitors had to go through the former store, where items were still on display. The performances were related thematically to the store, but the store was not really functioning as a set, having already been mostly dismantled. From his first Judson show on, Oldenburg has conceived of his exhi-

1.5
Rehearsal for Jim Dine's Happening, *Car Crash,* 1960 at the Reuben Gallery. Photograph by Robert R. McElroy.

bitions as "environment[s] in which all the elements were related thematically, stylistically and technically."[33]

One way the Environments of Dine, Oldenburg, and Kaprow were strongly related was in the use of junk materials. The aesthetics of "junk" dominated, as the artists aimed for a continuity between their works and everyday life. Kurt Schwitters had used junk, stating a desire to make "new art forms out of the remains of a former culture," but his detritus-filled collages were not intended to be thrown away.[34] For the Environment makers, the use of junk added to the ephemeral quality of their work. Many of the Environments were made of perishable materials such as newspaper, string, food, toilet paper, and adhesive tape. Not only would the whole thing be dismantled after the showing, but most of the time the individual components could not be salvaged in order to remake the piece. As Jim Dine said at the time:

I first started at the Reuben and at the Judson and it was all about junk. Finding things and putting them together. . . . I just figured that if you worked on it long enough it worked and if it didn't you threw it away. There was enough trash to make other things work . . . When my show [at the Reuben] was over I just threw most of it away. That's what almost everyone did that year.[35]

These materials gave the Environments a spontaneous, "expressionistic" quality and represent one of the aesthetic branches of Installation art that has continued to develop. A review of Kaprow's *An Apple Shrine* in the *Village Voice* described the Environment as "a modern labyrinth of narrow passageways constructed of chicken wire, ripped cardboard, rags, tarpaper, enormous quantities of torn and crumpled newspapers stuffed into the wire from ceiling to floor."[36]

The junk represented more than ephemeral, everyday material. It also communicated the message that this was a radically new art, nontraditional and nonprecious. In an era that celebrated American prosperity and consumerism, there was a critique implicit in the use of the throwaway remains and excesses of that culture. The use of junk could be seen as an assault on high art and the elite audience that it traditionally served.

Another similarity between Kaprow's Environments and those of Dine and Oldenburg was the use of the city itself as a source. Both Kaprow and Oldenburg articulated the desire to make an art that would have continuity with the physical environment outside the

1.6
Claes Oldenburg in *The Store*, New York, 1 December 1961 through 31 January 1962. Photograph by Robert R. McElroy.

gallery. Because the galleries with which they were involved tended to be downtown, on or near the Lower East Side, this meant bringing in the decrepit and entropic quality of these urban zones. Oldenburg proclaimed in 1961: "I am for the art of old plaster and new enamel. I am for the art of slag and black coal and dead birds. . . . I am for . . . the art of taxicabs. I am for the art of ice cream cones dropped on the street. I am for the majestic art of dogturds, rising like cathedrals. I am for the blinking arts, lighting up the night."[37] His enthusiasm for the milieu of the city found its way into his work.

Oldenburg, Kaprow, Dine, and Whitman worked to find places to show their Environments. These places contributed to the aesthetic of the works; moreover, without them, the works could not have been staged. The outlets were created out of necessity and provided what no other, more established place was offering at that time: an arena in which to experiment. New spaces had to open up that would allow the Environments not only to be seen, but to be constructed.

Kaprow felt very strongly that some of the new art needed new places for exhibition:

Gallery exhibited Environments almost invariably tend to be untouchable, static display pieces in conformity with the gallery tradition. All the marvelous potentials of transformation and interactivity between art, the public, and nature are out of the question. And even when a little of this is made possible, it is so tentative that the old habits of gallery-spectatorship preclude any vital response on the public's part, limit the work's duration to the standard three-week show, and do not prepare anyone for the idea that nature could ever be involved, much less welcomed.[38]

The Environments by Kaprow, Dine, Oldenburg, and Whitman were shown in alternative galleries including the Reuben Gallery and the Judson Gallery in New York. There was a lot of overlap between the activities at these spaces—Kaprow did a performance as part of the Ray-Gun activities organized by Oldenburg and Dine at Judson, for example.

The Judson Gallery was located in Judson Memorial Church at 239 Thompson Street, south of Washington Square Park, and was a small, noncommercial space. It was directed by Claes Oldenburg and Jim Dine beginning in 1960. The church had already been exhibiting art before this, including two-dimensional works by Oldenburg and Dine, but more radical things had begun to happen in the fall of 1959. Kaprow was also interested in the gallery, doing one Environment there and participating in one evening of performance. In a meeting with church administrators, Kaprow outlined his thoughts about the gallery:

Alan explains what the gallery means to him . . . The freedom to be free—"historically astonishing." . . .

What he has in mind
"Environments"—intensified interior or exterior—kind of intensified interior decoration Abstract Expressionism dead—need ways of expression growing. Go *IN* instead of LOOK *AT*.[39]

The minutes from this meeting also contain Kaprow's caution about fire hazards and the need for fire protection equipment: "Fire Hazard . . . must be constantly aware of danger."[40] For a brief period, Judson was the place where Environments and Happenings were taking place. But Dine, Kaprow, Oldenburg, and Robert Whitman eventually left Judson for a number of reasons. Kaprow says that it was partly because the program at Judson became explicitly political, which was a direction in which these particular artists did not want to go:

The church, under the direction of Al Carmines, became more involved with drug counseling and other services, and began to attract artists interested in a specific political statement. For example, Phyllis Yampolsky's *Hall of Issues* where people could put up statements that would then be discussed. [Jon Hendricks and Jean Toche] organized and sponsored more and more politically active work, sometimes quite aggressive, and that's one of the reasons why the original group there tended to move on, first of all helped by the more specific aesthetic concerns of the Reuben Gallery and then as one or the other artists moved to other places including uptown, it was a natural transition, might even have occurred if Judson had just simply burned down.[41]

In contrast to Kaprow, Oldenburg attributes his own leaving to the changing focus at Judson in terms of media—the art gallery gave way to the Judson Dance Theater:

It had nothing to do with their political agenda. They have phases where they concentrate on different areas. They concentrated on art, then a little bit later they shifted to music and dance. And then they had a political period. It depended who was in the church. Bud Scott emphasized music and literature. That was no problem with me that they had a political agenda.[42]

Dine said that one reason he left was the space. The space at Judson was just "a hole in the wall," and other places, like the Reuben Gallery, offered more. In addition, Dine recalls that he and Oldenburg did not want to continue to spend their time running a gallery. Attendance was another factor. The Judson Gallery did not attract many visitors. Dine remembers that *Rainbow Thoughts,* an Environment he built there that consisted of a black room with a blinking lightbulb and a tiny rainbow, received no visitors.[43] The Ray-Gun show was the only Judson exhibition with which he and Oldenburg were involved that was well attended.

The Ray-Gun show consisted of an Environment by Dine called *The House,* and one by Oldenburg called *The Street.* These were on exhibit during construction and continued to be on exhibit from 30 January to 19 February, 1960. Throughout the course of the exhibition, there were three evenings of performance—some of which took place in the Environments, some of which did not. Dine and Oldenburg participated in the performances, as did Kaprow, Al Hansen, Dick Higgins, Red Grooms, and Robert Whitman. With the exception of Dine and Oldenburg, none of the artists used *The House* or *The Street* as backdrops for their performances. Other spaces within the church were used, with the audience moving from room to room. The performances were billed under the collective name of Ray-Gun Spex. In a review of the Ray-Gun Spex in *Time,* Kaprow's role in the press as spokesperson is made evident:

One leader of the new movement is Allan Kaprow. . . . Kaprow's painting in the shape of a theater got started by way of giant paste-ups of indiscriminate materials. To bring back the idea of a picture, he hung canvas tatters in front of his paste-ups. Then he moved the tatters forward and installed lights behind them. Suddenly he had a stage, and so he brought on "happenings," something like the incidents children perform for an improvised circus. The idea took hold, and happenings have been put on around the world in the past year.[44]

The Hansa Gallery was another place where Environments were exhibited. One of the original artist-run cooperative galleries to open on East 10th Street in the 1950s, it was open from 1952 to 1959.[45] Although it had moved uptown to Central Park South in 1954, it still belonged downtown in spirit. Kaprow not only showed there but was one of the founding members, along with Robert Whitman and George Segal, among others. Although the Hansa Gallery had closed by the time Kaprow began publicly staging Happenings, the space was important as an early forum, and he showed his first Environment in its uptown location.

Richard Bellamy was the director of the Hansa Gallery at the time of its closing, and went on to found the Green Gallery in New York City in 1960.[46] In a 1963 interview with Richard Brown Baker, he discussed the importance of the Hansa Gallery and Kaprow's first Environment there:

Baker: Did Allan Kaprow have any thoughts that he could possibly sell that thing in connection with the exhibit? What was going on in his mind?

Bellamy: What was going on in Allan Kaprow's mind? Well okay, no, he had no thought to sell it. Nothing could be sold, nothing was purchasable in the exhibition. It was an environment. No one at that time or even now is prepared to purchase an environment by an artist. That is a work that encompasses the viewer. However I understand that Sidney Janis . . . is contemplating an exhibition of environments to take place in his new gallery space. . . . We would assume that if Mr. Janis were going to do this sort of thing that it would have definite commercial aspects. . . . I still don't think that any collector is prepared to purchase an environment as a work, certainly such a work as Allan Kaprow made then and much later developed into what is now known as Happenings. I do consider that it is important that Allan Kaprow did make this exhibition at the Hansa Gallery at that time. It has, as you say, historical importance. . . . There are certain judgements to make on Kaprow's work in general and on that exhibition, but I think that the important thing to note is that it did happen at the Hansa Gallery and it is the only place that it could have happened. It was the only existing gallery where an exhibition of that kind could have been put on.[47]

After the Hansa Gallery closed, Anita Reuben opened her Reuben Gallery, with Kaprow and George Segal among the Hansa Gallery artists who went on to show there. When the Reuben Gallery first opened in the fall of 1959, it was located at 61 Fourth Avenue, but later it moved to 44 East Third Street. In both locations, it was a site for exhibitions of Environments and also for Happenings by Kaprow and others. Kaprow's first public Happening, entitled *18 Happenings in 6 Parts,* was performed there.[48]

Also, Red Grooms founded the City Gallery and later the Delancey Street Museum, where he exhibited the work of Oldenburg, Dine, Lester Johnson, and others in the same circle.[49] None of these spaces were part of the commercial artworld, and this made them more open to showing experimental work. The exhibitions and events that took place in these spaces could not have happened anywhere else at the time. As Lawrence Alloway wrote in 1965 regarding the Reuben Gallery, "there was . . . an easy contact between the act of production and the act of presentation, which was very different from the regular marketing or promotional activities of art dealers."[50]

The Reuben Gallery and the Judson Gallery were ideal for the exhibiting of Environments because they were informal places where the artist could do what he pleased. At the same time, there was little consciousness of the possible physical dangers posed by environmental work, even if, in retrospect, there should have been. For example, Kaprow recalls worrying about his Environment *An Apple Shrine*—shown at Judson—being a firetrap. He even recalls spraying the newspapers with flame retardant. But the church officials expressed no concern.[51]

In addition to the spaces discussed above, artists exercised the option to create their own spaces. Claes Oldenburg's *Store,* for example, can be seen as a self-contained, alternative exhibition space.

None of Kaprow's Environments was originally presented in a museum. Kaprow was against museums in principle, for he saw them as responsible for isolating and separating art from daily life. He had a clearly articulated antimuseum stance. His antagonism toward the museum as an institution did not take the form of trying to change the museum or subvert it from within. Instead, for a long time, he bypassed it altogether.[52] Kaprow was a purist. In the heyday of his creation of Environments and Happenings, he found spaces at further and further remove from the established art venues. In 1962 he accepted a commission for a performance by the Walker Art

Museum, but the performance was actually staged in the Lehmann mushroom caves in St. Paul.

Kaprow came close to showing one of his Environments at a major New York museum in 1963, when the Museum of Modern Art organized a circulating exhibition entitled *Hans Hofmann and His Students.* The exhibition included works by fifty artists who had studied with Hofmann. When William Seitz invited Kaprow to participate, his only stipulations were that the piece "be something that demonstrates your interpretation of Hofmann's ideas, and is reasonably practical for exhibitors to present."[53] Kaprow's contribution was entitled *Push and Pull: A Furniture Comedy for Hans Hofmann.* The "work" was a series of instructions, Kaprow's intention being that the finished product would look different in each of the venues. In its traveling form, the piece consisted of a crate containing twenty-six cardboard placards on which Kaprow had written instructions about building an Environment, and thirty-six blank sheets on which viewers/participants could write. The placards could be removed from the crate and read by the visitors. Visitors could also add text to the blank placards provided by the artist. The push and pull in Kaprow's title was a dig at Hofmann's widely quoted theory that in painting, if there is one shape "pushing," there must be another that is "pulling." The push and pull in Kaprow's piece referred to the physical activity of moving furniture. It would be the first Environment Kaprow had done that was shown in a museum rather than in an alternative space.

Before the exhibition went on tour, the Museum of Modern Art hosted a special preview of the whole show, including Kaprow's piece, at the Santini warehouse in Long Island City, where the exhibition had been assembled to be packed. William Seitz felt it would be an appropriate venue for Kaprow's Environment because it was an unhistoricized, nonaesthetic space—Kaprow agreed.[54] His piece was given top billing in the press release and invitation. Attendees of the warehouse preview included Alfred Barr, Brian O'Doherty, and Richard Bellamy, others.

Kaprow had constructed the Environment at the warehouse himself, using two separate rooms. The visitors were invited to rearrange the furniture in the spaces. On the tour, Kaprow would not be involved at all with assembling the piece. Part of the point of the piece was that each exhibitor could do it differently, based on Kaprow's general instructions. Kaprow had sent a letter to all the exhibitors saying, "Each exhibitor has the right to set up the Environment-Happening or disregard it. Either he may do it himself or appoint some person to do it for him. . . . Somewhere nearby could be displayed photos of the piece as it was arranged in New York City, and also those taken of each new version of it. . . . I am most interested in the handshake between the artist and others. The museum or gallery director can now be instrumental in bringing this about."[55]

The Museum of Modern Art circulated *Hans Hofmann and His Students* to fifteen venues between May 1963 and March 1965. Most of the venues were university art galleries, including the Indiana University Museum of Art and the Lowe Art Museum in Miami. None of the venues were in the New York vicinity. In terms of Kaprow's piece, things did not go according to his plan. Despite his instructions, not one venue constructed an Environment, and in some cases the box of placards was simply exhibited as a piece of sculpture, on a pedestal with other sculptures. Kaprow wrote of the whole experience: "From reports, I gather that this arrangement [of the Environment-Happening] has not worked out optimally. In an exhibition atmosphere people are not geared to enter into the process of art. Hence, this kind of work is much better off away from the habits and rituals of conventional culture."[56]

Being away from the habits and rituals of conventional culture had its problems as well. Spaces such as the Judson Gallery or the Reuben Gallery were off the beaten path and their shows undervisited. Publicity was scant and critical attention was both slight and slighting. Environments were a new form, the use of junk as art material was also new (or at least its revival was), and the apparent "free-for-all" atmosphere generated by visitors to the Environments was new and unfamiliar as well. All of these factors contributed to a negative critical response. Jim Dine recalls:

One of the things that upset me always about the response [to Environments], and of course one can never determine what the response is going to be or control it really, was that everybody just thought it was so god-damned funny. It was just so much fun. . . . They wouldn't have said that about a painting.[57]

It is true that by and large the critics did not know what to make of the Environments, and often resorted to a kind of tongue-in-cheek philistinism. But even while they were poking fun, they focused on the participatory nature of the work; it was the central, critical issue. They did not necessarily like it, but they addressed it. Their responses established some of the issues, although not the tone, that would continue to characterize the responses to room-size works of art.

As Dine observed, few critics made serious efforts to understand the work; rather, they would use a bastardization of Kaprow's theory as a substitute for real inquiry. The reviews tended to focus on the reviewer's own participation in—or experience of—the piece. For example, regarding Kaprow's Judson Environment *An Apple Shrine,* reviewed in *Art News:* "It's a place to be alone. It's like staring at forbidden fruit. Anyway, it's someplace about which feelings rush in where thoughts wouldn't be caught dead."[58] And of Dine's *Rainbow Thoughts,* also at Judson: "It is really a place to go and empty your mind. . . . 'Now what,' you think, or 'so what,' and then words fail, and thoughts also."[59] The nature of these comments reflects the non-traditional aspects of Environments. A glance at reviews of exhibitions in traditional media in those same issues of *Art News* reveals the predominance of primarily objective descriptions. In the reviews of Environments, the approach switches to a subjective point of view. This demonstrates the potential for an Environmental situation to inspire the viewer to examine his or her own perceptions of and reactions to the situation. A narrative describing an individual's experience replaces the disassociated tone of formal analysis, which appears to have been deemed inadequate for discussing Environments.

Often the writing itself is done in a stream of consciousness way, apparently in response to the spontaneous appearance of the Environments themselves. For example, again regarding *An Apple Shrine,* one critic wrote. "The haloed shapes recall the baby cry from the cradle protected by the electric eye at the world's fair. The stillness is a ghost town evacuated at that moment before an avalanche."[60] Few of the reviews tried to grapple with all the challenging implications of Environments as an art form. One exception was a review of *An Apple Shrine* in the *Village Voice,* written by Theodore Tucker, a Massachusetts-based critic who had seen the show in New York. He suggests some of the things about the Environment in general that are problematic:

Admittedly, Mr. Kaprow's art poses problems. The exhibition is now dismantled, its materials have been carted away by the junkman, and it will not be seen again. If its vocabulary is unfamiliar, it will not remain to be judged at a later, more knowledgeable year. Its life is a present one, and only memory can carry it into the future. . . . There is a distrust and fear of an expression which is short-lived by intention, as though this were subtly calling upon death itself. One cannot comprehend an attitude which bluntly embraces the fleeting. Perishable materials, perishable forms, perishable genius; chance, change—all conspire to damn this work and dissolve our values. Far beyond the "Apple Shrine's" actual content and humanity stands Kaprow's inadvertent quarrel with all the vapid glories, qualities and eternities which we think are History.[61]

This review is unique in its thoughtfulness and willingness to look seriously at the Environment and consider its wider implications, something that most reviewers did not do at this time. Tucker identifies some of the fundamental issues that have made, and continue to make, this art form difficult to historicize.

Critical response to the Ray-Gun show, which received scant coverage, was mixed; however, Suzanne Kiplinger, writing for the *Village Voice,* made the following prophetic statement:

I honestly feel that this form—that of art enveloping the viewer—might go places. Like many new forms, it seems excessively wild at the moment, but the artists involved are making their guide-posts as they go along and undoubtedly will refine and simplify as they go.[62]

Initially there was hostility to the idea of the viewer having to become more active. In a review in *Art News* of Kaprow's Environment at the Hansa Gallery in 1958, the reviewer wrote: "The spectator enters the exhibition [to quote from Kaprow's statement] 'according to his talents for engagement', also 'a much greater responsibility is placed on the visitor than he has had before.' If the visitor is not entertained, he is guilty of irresponsibility."[63] By the time of the *Words* exhibition in 1962, the notion of the viewer participating had become somewhat more acceptable, but only somewhat. A review of *Words* in *Art News* in 1962 stated: "An Environment resembles a Happening . . . in that in both the public becomes part of the action. The big difference between the two is the time element. An Environment is unconcentrated, a prolonged presentation for the convenience and edification of the public, which pays fifty cents a head for the privilege of being part of one."[64] The reviewer makes a generalization about what an Environment is, based on Kaprow's piece, and this definition includes the idea that the public is part of the action—the viewer is a participant. Being part of the Environment was considered both its selling point and its problem. It was sometimes seen as something positive: a democratic attempt to engage the viewer in a way that differed from previous expectations of experiencing art. And it was sometimes seen as threatening or merely irritating. Also, the temporal aspects of the viewing experience were stressed; it takes time to see (experience) one. The implications of the temporal in an art-viewing situation would become more central later in the decade with the modernist critique of Minimalism and, by extension, related endeavors such as Installation art.

Some of the strongest negative criticism came when Environments were first shown in a more established context than the alternative downtown spaces. The Martha Jackson Gallery (located at 32 East Sixty-ninth Street) was showing artists from the Judson Gallery and the Reuben Gallery by 1960. Although in general the gallery showed avant-garde painting, Martha Jackson was willing, during a brief period, to show radical art in other media as well. This was demonstrated by the two exhibitions *New Media—New Forms in Painting and Sculpture, Part I* and *Part II,* that were held there in 1960. Although no Environments were included in these two landmark exhibitions, junk assemblage was presented. Kaprow wrote the catalog essay for the first of the two shows. In May 1961 the gallery went even further out on a limb, inviting six artists to create Environments in situ. The resulting exhibition, *Environments, Situations, Spaces,* was important for many reasons, despite a general lack of enthusiasm in the press. According to Oldenburg, the show was so unfamiliar that no one could even see it (register it).[65] The artists who participated were George Brecht, Jim Dine, Walter Gaudnek, Allan Kaprow, Claes Oldenburg, and Robert Whitman. Despite its location, the exhibition did not have the effect of validating Environments as an artform, at least from the critical perspective. As one critic wrote:

The "terrible children" invaded Martha Jackson's Gallery last May and June with more of those baffling non-commercial commodities, things you can't use or sell or label even, which nobody could be too clear about why they should be encouraged or endured much less considered the prestige items they obviously are, or else why would Miss Jackson (whose commercial acumen is well known) clutter up her fashionable yard with a bunch of junky car tires that she permitted Alan Kaprow to put there?[66]

Martha Jackson, on the other hand, felt the exhibition had been a success, as she said in an interview with Paul Cummings in 1969:

The following June we had Environments, Situations, Spaces. We divided the gallery into six sections and we gave a section to each of six artists. It was not as successful as the first show but it was the first show uptown of Environments. And it led to many museum shows afterwards where they did the same thing; they divided the museum up and gave each artist a section. . . . I think it's the last show where a gallery could lead a museum. Now they don't want any gallery to get ahead of them.[67]

The exhibition challenged the gallery as well as its visitors on many levels. Regarding *Yard*, Kaprow's entry in *Environments, Situations, Spaces*, Jackson said to Cummings in retrospect:

Jackson: We were so afraid that some girl would trip on her high heels walking on the tires. I went abroad as usual, and my son was here. And the people next door called the fire department and made a complaint. So we were asked to go to court. My son got hold of a lawyer and went to court and was fined. The lawyer got him off but charged as much as the fine or something. . . .

Cummings: What was the reason? Because the tires were a fire hazard or something?

Jackson: No, they're not a fire hazard. But maybe they were an escape hazard. . . . Maybe they felt that firemen couldn't get in here if there was a fire. Some ordinance. . . . But they didn't know what was happening; they didn't realize it was a show. [68]

The press release issued by the gallery for *Environments, Situations, Spaces* described the new work as follows:

The exhibition . . . is unique in that it is the first group show by artists working within the totality of physical space creating environments which demand full and active participation from the viewer. . . .Each artist [Brecht, Dine, Gaudnek, Kaprow, Oldenburg, Whitman], though highly individual, aims at complete utilization of all facets of environmental space; achieving, thereby, a new and profound form of art expression. Walls, ceilings and floors lose their confining identity, merging into this recreated space. The viewer finds himself within the artistic statement, forcing him to forgo his passive objectivity. [69]

The selling point of the exhibition was the notion of the audience as participant, which was played up as a positive element in the work. By this time, from the critical perspective, this idea was inseparable from the definition of an Environment. Once again, Kaprow functioned as spokesperson: "As Allan Kaprow . . . explained it last week, 'We invite people to cast aside their proper manners and partake wholly of art and life. They must not be afraid to get dirty.' " [70] In fact, the degree of participatory experience available to the viewer varied from piece to piece, as did the degree to which the artists actually constructed Environments.

There is an eyewitness account of Gaudnek's piece, *Unlimited Dimensions,* that vividly invokes the experience of being in it, demonstrating the importance of the first-person experience in looking at this work, and the potential for the work to exercise and sharpen our own perceptions. Brian O'Doherty describes being in the piece as follows:

And then I stumbled into something worthwhile.

This is a dark little house made up of acutely angled corridors twilit by hidden torches. On the walls are vast targets with bullseyes cut out, so that one can look across and through the interior anatomy of the building. Using this strictly limited means, many delusions are produced. One enters a fragile little cosmos that requires a constant refocusing of the eyes. Gentle

1./
Installation view of
Claes Oldenburg's
The Store and Robert
Whitman's *Untitled*
in *Environments,
Situations, Spaces,*
Martha Jackson
Gallery, New York,
1961. Photograph
courtesy Poetry/Rare
Books Collection,
University Libraries,
State University of
New York at Buffalo.

refractions require double and triple takes. And it is all done without mirrors.[71]

All of the artists had been invited to make an Environment, but they did not all do this. George Brecht's entry was a single white wicker chair that could be moved around or sat in. Oldenburg's piece was also not an Environment (figure 1.7). Regarding the evolution of his piece in the show, he said:

And so the original idea for the Martha Jackson Gallery show was that it was to be a room and that these pieces were to be a sort of total environment. They were supposed to hang so closely together that it would be all like a grotto full of these pieces. . . . And of course Kaprow came in and dumped all these tires in the back yard and everyone got very frightened. So the way it turned out I just hung these things on a wall very close together and made a kind of mural. . . . And then it was as a result of the fact that it hadn't been realized there that I set about redoing it as an environment. Which led to the store that became The Store downtown. And I rented that store in the course of 1961, I think it was June or something. So that was a direct result of the Jackson show.[72]

As far as the few critics who covered the show were concerned, *Environments, Situations, Spaces* was taken as lightly as if it had been shown at the Judson or Reuben Gallery. *Art News's* Jack Kroll covered the exhibition in just a few sentences. His opening sentence, " 'Situations and Environments' offered the Happenings Boys in some more attempts to create Innocence using the methods of Franken-stein," sums up his response.[73] Brian O'Doherty, writing for the *New York Times,* found the exhibition only slightly more substantial: "All of this is based on a perfectly reasonable premise—that the sculptor can shape the environment to the human scale, and then release us inside it to walk around and add to our experiences." But he expressed disappointment that the artists appeared to take what they had done seriously. Obviously, O'Doherty did not. The one exception he made was for Gaudnek.

In January 1964, the exhibition *Four Environments by Four New Realists* was held at the Sidney Janis Gallery. At the time, this gallery symbolized established Fifty-seventh Street status. The artists included were Jim Dine, Claes Oldenburg, George Segal, and James Rosenquist, who were all on the rise and were by this time identified as Pop artists.

From the critical perspective, the exhibition was considered a failure across the board. It was unanimously disliked but for a variety of reasons. Some critics who were already hostile to Pop art disliked it on the same grounds as they disliked Pop—that it presented, but failed to interpret, everyday life. Other critics disliked the exhibition because the works presented failed to conform to their definition of an Environment. The exhibition might have been received with less hostility had it been called something else. In fact, Carroll Janis recalls that he had originally wanted to call it "Environmental Art," which implied something more general, but Sidney Janis chose to use "Environments" because it was a catchy term. The gallery was aware that the works in the exhibition were not Environments, and was not trying to enlarge upon the definition by labeling them thus.[74] But this is not the spirit in which the works were received.

Gene Swenson found Oldenburg's contribution to the exhibition, *Bedroom Ensemble* (figure 1.8), to be a disaster as an Environment, in part because "the gallery compounded the error [of the piece] by chaining off the room to make us look at it rather than letting us sense it."[75] In fact, it was Oldenburg's decision that the piece be roped off so people could not enter. He felt the whole effect of the piece would be lost if people walked through it.[76] By contrast, Barbara Rose found that "the only successful environment at Janis was Oldenburg's."[77] In a review for the *New York Times,* John Canaday found Segal's tableau and Oldenburg's *Bedroom Ensemble* to be the only "true environments" in the exhibition. Rosenquist's entry invited audience participation in a manner more consistent with Environments shown downtown, but Canaday described one of Rosenquist's entries as follows: "Something untitled, lying on the floor . . . which is a construction of horizontal Plexiglas panels crossed by wooden slat bridges, which you could probably walk across, plus more light bulbs.

1.8
Claes Oldenburg,
Bedroom Ensemble,
1963. Wood, vinyl,
metal, artificial fur,
cloth, and paper.
17 x 21 feet.
National Gallery of
Canada, Ottawa.

As far as I was concerned, these exhibits were crudely executed affairs devoid of environmental suggestion or any other kind of stimulus." Environment, in Canaday's book, does not require spectator involvement as a criterion. This is borne out in his description of the George Segal tableau: "At one end of an otherwise black-walled chamber, George Segal has erected a full-scale Plexiglas-and-metal sign, illuminated from behind, with a life-size plaster figure in front of it. . . . The effect is altogether eerie—completely realistic and matter-of-fact in detail, but spectral, sinister and paralyzed in a kind of desperate airlessness. This is an environment indeed."[78]

A clear distinction exists between an Environment and tableaux such as Segal's. Kaprow used the term "Environmental Sculpture" to describe Segal's work, indicating its difference from an Environment. But in Canaday's review, the term "Environment" simply refers to the space occupied by a discrete work. Dore Ashton dismissed the title of the exhibition entirely: "Of course [Four Environments] is only a convenient title, for it is impossible to create an environment in an art gallery, which already has an overwhelming environment of its own."[79]

By the time the exhibition *Four Environments by Four New Realists* opened at the Sidney Janis Gallery, there was no longer a need for Oldenburg or Dine to show at off-the-beaten path spaces, as they had acquired gallery representation. Meanwhile, the Judson Gallery had moved on to focus on music and dance. The Hansa and Reuben Galleries were closed. Martha Jackson had not followed through on the promise of the three radical exhibitions she had staged in 1960 and 1961. Kaprow was exclusively committed to the Happening, and was doing his Happenings far away from the institutions of the art world.

1.9
Yayoi Kusama, *One Thousand Boats Show*, 1964, Gertrude Stein Gallery, New York, 1964. Courtesy Robert Miller Gallery, New York. Photograph by Rudolph Burckhardt. © Yayoi Kusama.

1.10
Lucas Samaras,
Room #1, 1964.
Mixed media,
10 x 15 x 7½ feet.
Recreation of the
interior of Lucas
Samaras's bedroom
(detail). Installed at
the Green Gallery,
New York, 1964.
Photograph
by Wes Russell,
courtesy of Pace
Wildenstein.

In addition to the *Four Environments by Four New Realists* exhibition, individual Environments were occasionally presented in galleries around New York City. Yayoi Kusama's *One Thousand Boats* Environment was shown at the Gertrude Stein Gallery in 1964 (figure 1.9). She filled the gallery with images of a rowboat covered with small, white appendages. In the center of the room stood the actual boat. In September of 1964 Lucas Samaras transferred the contents of a room that had served as both his living quarters and his studio for fourteen years into the Green Gallery. The six-by-thirteen-foot room contained his bed, clothing, books, and manuscripts and an array of objects such as one might find in a studio (figure 1.10). Entitled *Room #1,* it was offered for sale at $17,000. Samaras was quoted in a *New York Times* review as saying, "I see [the piece] as assemblage, even sculpture. It is my past, complete—a piece of biography—the realest thing I could do."[80] Samaras would continue investigating the possibilities of room-size works of art in a more abstract vein, with *Room #2,* a mirrored room exhibited at the Pace Gallery in 1966. In the spring of 1966, Andy Warhol installed his *Cow Wallpaper* and *Silver Clouds* at the Leo Castelli Gallery. But the continuing discourse on participation in a work of art would not center on the work of these artists. It would center on a circle of New York artists who became known as Minimalists.

CHAPTER 2

Situations

In the early 1960s, new forms were developed and new terms proposed that are an important part of Installation art's history. Although not all of the sculpture that came to be known as Minimalism relates to the Installation art idea as described thus far, a significant portion of it does. Important theoretical issues raised by some of the artists associated with Minimalism and by contemporaneous critics are germane to Installation art. Of particular significance was the focus on the relationship between the spectator—now sometimes referred to as the beholder—and the work of art. The work of art was often regarded as part of a situation rather than divorced from it. As Installation art moved toward greater critical attention, the work of Robert Morris and Donald Judd, as well as Carl Andre, Dan Flavin, and others would become part of the picture, defining anew the terms of the genre.

Minimalism was initially referred to by a number of different names, including primary structures, ABC art, and literalism. The term "Minimalism" was originated by the British philosopher Richard Wollheim, who used it in 1965 to identify art that he saw as having minimal art content because it was so close to raw materials or existing images.[1] As with many terms in the history of art, Minimalism has been applied to artists whose sensibilities were in fact quite different from each other. Minimalism has been used to describe nonreferential geometric sculpture, but while artists might share that aesthetic, they can come to it from quite different directions. To give but one example, Tony Smith created "minimal" sculpture using large, abstract geometric forms. Smith's artistic sensibility was akin to that of the Abstract Expressionists, with their belief in metaphor and intuition, and the primary role of these elements in artmaking.[2] Robert Morris also constructed large geometric forms (in addition to making other kinds of objects), but he was fundamentally interested in how the viewer perceived and interacted with the work—how the viewer went about "knowing an object."[3] How Minimalism is defined dictates who is included under its aegis. A general history of modern art defines Minimalism in formal terms as "sculpture that creates an architectural space or environment."[4] This definition has limitations because it does not take into account the viewer's role. But the notion of Minimalism as having the ability to create an environment has important ramifications for Installation art. Kenneth Baker offers a philosophical designation when he talks of Minimalism as "the drive to clarify the terms in which art takes a place in the world."[5] This, too, relates to the Installation art idea, with a focus on the role of the spectator.

The meaning of spectator participation that emerged around Minimalism in the early 1960s varied from artist to artist, at times revolving around the situation in which the work of art was placed. Robert Morris's three L-beams, identical but for their orientation in space, require the beholder to be aware of his or her own role in knowing the work. Measure for measure, all three beams are identical, however, they are perceived as different from one another because of their orientation (figure 2.1). In a viewing situation, both the sameness of the forms and the awareness of their difference is experienced—simultaneously or sequentially. There is a time factor involved in this unveiling, and a participatory factor as the viewer confronts the objects. The individual's experience of the work and the questions the work might raise regarding the nature of art constitute participation.

By the time of the first major museum exhibition of Minimalism, the issue of spectator participation in relation to the new sculpture was present. *Primary Structures: Work by Younger British and American Sculptors* was held at the Jewish Museum in 1966. At the time, the Jewish Museum was a fitting venue for a pioneering exhibition of avant-garde art. Under the direction of Alan Solomon until 1965, and subsequently Sam Hunter, the Jewish Museum established itself in the 1960s as a venue for avant-garde exhibitions, holding early shows of the work of Robert Rauschenberg, Jasper Johns, and Jim Dine. Many of the artists included in *Primary Structures* would ultimately be identified with Minimalism, including Morris, Carl

2.1
Robert Morris, *Untitled (Three L-Beams)*, 1969 refabrication of 1965 original. Painted plywood, three units, each 96 x 96 x 24 inches (243.8 x 243.8 x 61 cm). Photograph courtesy of the Solomon R. Guggenheim Museum, New York. © Robert Morris Archives. © 1999 Artists Rights Society (ARS), New York.

Andre, Judd, and Flavin. These artists had already had individual gallery exhibitions. A number of New York galleries, including the Green Gallery, Dwan Gallery, Tibor de Nagy, and Castelli Galleries, were early venues for the new sculpture. Minimalism did not spend a long time at the margin of the art world. In fact, by 1968, as Barbara Haskell relates, "The dominance of this so-called reductive work was so great that John Perrault reported a rumor that many galleries were refusing any art that was not Minimal or could not disguise itself as Minimal."[6]

Kynaston McShine was the curator of *Primary Structures*. In his brief catalog introduction, he addressed, among other issues, the role of the spectator and the importance of the relationship between the work and the surrounding space: "The generally large scale of the work and its architectural proportions allow the sculpture to dominate the environment. At times the sculpture intrudes aggressively on the spectator's space, or the spectator is drawn into sculptural space. Often the structure acts ambiguously, creating a spatial dislocation for the spectator with complex meanings." And in conclusion, "The new sculptors are transforming contemporary aesthetics. . . . Their work demands our attention and active participation."[7] His words hint at the complexity of the critical response to Minimalism, which had already begun to engage with the larger implications of this art. Both critics and artists contributed to the discourse.

Donald Judd was a prolific and articulate writer, and reviewed some of the early exhibitions of Minimalism, even as he was creating some of its strongest visual statements. His 1965 article, "Specific Objects," suggested that works need not bear a relationship to the space in which they were installed: "Obviously, anything in three dimensions can be any shape, regular or irregular, and can have any relation to the wall, floor, ceiling, room, rooms or exterior or none at all."[8] For Judd, it was certainly not a requirement that an environmental situation be created—although one might be perceived. For instance, critic Michael Benedikt described Judd's work in a 1966 group show at the Dwan Gallery in environmental terms: "Although grayish, the row of six-foot high galvanized iron boxes by Judd also seemed to sculpt space outward, throwing as much interest on the space around it as it attracted to itself."[9] Judd believed that each element in one of his works was equally important and autonomous, whether it had one unit or several. Even a single-unit piece can raise the question of the relationship of the object to its surrounding space. *Untitled*, 1965 is a large piece of perforated steel that sits directly on the floor of an exhibition space and must be navigated around. The viewer must decide how close to the piece to come—in effect, deciding how much space is claimed by the object (figure 2.2). *Untitled*, 1968, invites the viewer to move around its five sections (figure 2.3).

2.2
Donald Judd, *Untitled*, 1965. Perforated steel, 8 x 120 x 66 inches (20.3 x 304.8 x 167.6 cm.) Collection of Whitney Museum of American Art. Fiftieth Anniversary Gift of Toiny and Leo Castelli. Photograph © 1999: Whitney Museum of American Art. © Estate of Donald Judd/licensed by VAGA, New York.

In a series of articles published in *Artforum* beginning in 1966, Robert Morris discussed the triad of sculpture, space and viewer. He specified that his intent does not lie in creating an environment, in that it is not the space itself that has been designed:

For the space of the room itself is a structuring factor both in its cubic shape and in terms of the kinds of compression different sized and proportioned rooms can effect upon the object-subject terms. That the space of the room becomes of such importance does not mean that an environmental situation is being established. The total space is hopefully altered in certain desired ways by the presence of the object. It is not controlled in the sense of being ordered by an aggregate of objects or by some shaping of the space surrounding the viewer.[10]

Morris's exhibition at the Green Gallery in 1964 (figure 2.4) incorporated the space of the gallery into the work. Seven different elements were included that related to the space of the gallery in dif-

2.3
Donald Judd, *Untitled*, 1968. Five open rectangles of painted steel, each $48\frac{3}{8}$ inches x 10 feet x $20\frac{1}{4}$ inches; overall, $48\frac{3}{8}$ x 10 feet x 10 feet 1 inch. The Museum of Modern Art, New York. Mr. and Mrs. Simon Askin Fund. Photograph © 1999 The Museum of Modern Art. © Estate of Donald Judd/licensed by VAGA, New York.

ferent ways. To name just two, *Untitled (Corner Beam)* was installed so that it spanned a corner of the gallery, while *Untitled (Cloud)* was suspended from the ceiling.

Morris's 1964 Green Gallery exhibition bears out the above remarks. It was reviewed by Judd, who also did not find it to be environmental: "The work looks well together, but it isn't an environment; there are seven separate pieces. If Morris made an environment, it would certainly be one thing."[11] At the same time, neither Judd's nor Morris's Minimal sculptures are strictly autonomous objects. When exhibited, they become part of a situation that also includes the space and the viewer.

The situational aspect of Minimal sculpture is also borne out in the work of Carl Andre. Andre's floor pieces emphasize the relationship of the work to the floor, and also challenge the spectator to consider that relationship. If the work is perceived as an object, then it ought not to be walked on. If it is continuous with the floor, as with a rug, it can be walked on. But the viewer is trained not to touch, let alone step on sculpture. Viewers interacted with Andre's *144 Lead Square,* 1969 at the Museum of Modern Art (figure 2.5) as follows: timidly at first, self-consciously, the viewer steps on, stands on, smirks guiltily, and finally walks on the piece, participating in the challenge to sculpture as well as the challenge to proper museum behavior.

Dan Flavin used light to create environments that the spectator could enter. He first showed his neon tube sculpture at the Green Gallery in 1963. His work reflects his interest in using technology and industrial materials (neon tubing) to create a work of art. The light creates an environment, and is ephemeral in the sense that all one need do is switch it off for it to vanish entirely. Light has the ability to define a space, but not everyone responded to the environmental aspect of Flavin's work. In response to an exhibition of Flavin's work in 1965, Jacob Grosberg merely wrote: "There are seven pieces in the show. Fixtures are arranged in various sequences. They are of varying sizes, and have different-colored fluorescent tubes."[12]

An environmental quality was perceived by some critics in gallery exhibitions of Minimalist sculpture. Regarding an exhibition by Michael Steiner at the Dwan Gallery, Benedikt wrote: "The strangeness of [the show], and other American primary shows (including those of Morris and Judd) stems from the fact that the

Figure 2.4
Robert Morris, Exhibition at the Green Gallery, New York, December 1964–January 1965. Photograph courtesy of the Solomon R. Guggenheim Museum, New York. © Robert Morris Archives. © 1999 Artists Rights Society (ARS), New York.

effect of the whole show tends to be more than the sum of its parts: seen *en groupe* there is an air of the mysterious, even of the environmental. . . . American primary work is distinguished from the best current British sculpture by its mysteriously environmental quality." He goes on to describe an exhibition at the Cordier-Eckstrom gallery of Walter de Maria's work: "De Maria's environment would appear to be more or less theatrical."[13] He suggests in a later note that there is "a convergence of the Happening and Architecturalist esthetic."[14] The focus on the viewing situation, or the whole space as affecting the art experience emerges as a central critical issue later that same year.

"Environmental" gave way to "theatrical" in 1967. Theatricality was the central issue of the seminal work of Minimalist critique of the decade, Michael Fried's article "Art and Objecthood," which appeared in *Artforum* in June 1967. Fried, a modernist critic, faulted Minimalism for its theatricality. Theatricality was the term he gave to the temporal and interactive aspects he perceived in the work of Judd and Morris, which he grouped together. For Fried, theatricality was a negative trait, for it implied that the pure categories of painting and

2.5
Carl Andre, *144 Lead Square,* 1969. 144 lead plates, each approx. $\frac{3}{8}$ x 12 x 12 inches. Museum of Modern Art, New York. Advisory Committee Fund. Photograph © 1999 The Museum of Modern Art, New York.

sculpture had been violated: there was now another discipline, theater, that fell outside the domain of both. "Good" modernist art was not theatrical.

According to Fried, Minimalist art (or literalist, as he referred to it) does not transcend the condition of non-art; it is merely an object that requires a duration of time to behold and places too much emphasis on the beholder and the space in which the work exists. In fact, it is dependent on the beholder and the space—in other words, the situation. By contrast, good modernist art does not require a situation for its successful completion. It exists no matter what the viewing scenario. Fried found the work of British sculptor Anthony Caro to be modernist. The distinction that Fried drew between Caro on one hand and Morris and Judd on the other had not been drawn in *Primary Structures*, which included works by all three.

There are several ideas in Fried's article that are of particular significance to the study of Installation art. The first is the notion of Minimal sculpture as creating a situation. Relying heavily on the work and words of Robert Morris, Fried wrote, "Literalist sensibility is theatrical because, to begin with, it is concerned with the actual circumstances in which the beholder confronts literalist work." Even though Fried is responding to individual works of sculpture, he describes an effect which transcends the object when he says, "The beholder knows himself to stand in an indeterminate, open-ended—and unexacting—relation as *subject* to the impassive object on the wall or floor. In fact, being distanced by such objects is not . . . entirely unlike being distanced, or crowded by the silent presence of another *person*; the experience of coming upon a literalist object unexpectedly —for example, in somewhat darkened rooms—can be strongly, if momentarily disquieting in just this way." [15] Although Fried used the idea of theatricality in an attempt to discredit Minimalism, his essay confirmed some of the aims of Minimalism. As Barbara Haskell points out, Fried's "view that the art had the quality of a 'situation' unintentionally affirmed Minimalism's success in visually engaging the spectator." [16]

Fried also found literalist art to have a temporal quality: "Endlessness, being able to go on and on, even having to go on and on . . . seems to be the experience that most deeply excites literalist sensibility, and which literalist artists seek to objectify in their work." [17] This is in contrast to modernist painting or sculpture, which can be grasped instantaneously, while literalist art is perceived over time. Temporality, the idea of the work revealing itself over time, is a factor for Installation art. Art on a room scale must be explored and traversed to be grasped, and that exploration, however brief, takes time.

Although Fried is talking about abstract sculpture, theatricality, as he defines it, is a link between artists who have different aesthetics, ranging from abstract to pictorial. Fried notes in "Art and Objecthood" that "it is theatricality, too, that links [Judd, Morris, Andre, Sol LeWitt, Tony Smith, Ronald Bladen, Robert Grosvenor] to other figures as disparate as Kaprow, Cornell, Rauschenberg, Oldenburg, Kienholz, Segal, Samaras, Christo, Kusama . . . the list could go on indefinitely." [18] To apply Fried's arguments in retrospect to Kaprow, Oldenburg, and Dine; the easy move these artists made from Environments to Happenings; and their use of some Environments as stage sets for Happenings underscores the inherent theatricality (as a positive trait) of their endeavors. In the wake of

Fried's article, theatricality blossomed. As Fried himself has recently acknowledged: "No one with even the sketchiest awareness of recent history needs to be told that 'theatricality,' not just in the form of Minimalism, went on to flourish spectacularly while abstraction in my sense of the term became more and more beleaguered."[19] Regarding "Art and Objecthood," he reflects that "my essay is nowhere near as pessimistic as future events would warrant from my point of view; I don't seem to have imagined the possibility that within a few years the art I admired would be all but submerged under an avalanche of more or less openly theatrical productions and practices, as proved to be the case."[20] Fried is referring to Body art, Performance art, and video art, all of which flourished over the next decade. Installation art exists in this context as well.

Another important part of the critical response to Minimalism that has significant bearing on Installation art is the discussion of phenomenology that entered the literature beginning in 1968. Starting with Annette Michelson, critics including Rosalind Krauss, Marcia Tucker, and Robert Morris discussed Minimal sculpture in phenomenological terms. The work of a number of different philosophers, including Ludwig Wittgenstein, Charles Pierce, and Maurice Merleau-Ponty, was used to illuminate the Minimal sculptures of Robert Morris and, to a lesser extent, Donald Judd and some of the work of Bruce Nauman and Richard Serra, among others. Merleau-Ponty's *Phenomenology of Perception* was translated from French in 1962 and provided a fascinating basis for approaching art as lived experience.[21] As Krauss stated, "The *Phenomenology of Perception* became, in the hands of the Americans, a text that was consistently interpreted in the light of their own ambitions toward meaning within an art that was abstract." [22] In the context of a discussion of Richard Serra's *Shift*, 1970–72, Krauss said, "This is not to say that *Shift* has Merleau-Ponty's text as anything like a specific 'source' or direct influence. Rather, almost ten years of general absorption of these ideas developed an American context in which sculpture lived in a play of perspectives, as in the minimalist work of Donald Judd or Robert Morris, where abstract geometries are constantly submitted to the definition of a sited vision." The notion of a sited vision places emphasis on the beholders and their experience, or perspective, that is, "the activity of the viewer's relationship to his world." [23] Krauss's words offer a clear and straightforward view of how phenomenology can be used to illuminate certain works of art. Another clear example is Maurice Berger's description of the effect of Morris's baseless sculptures installed directly on the gallery floor: "Rather than approaching allusive, rarefied forms, the viewer could now walk along, around, and even through the sculpture—a situation that emphasized the phenomenological implications of time and physical passage." [24]

Phenomenology was not only drawn into the service of interpreting abstract works. In *PheNAUMANology*, Marcia Tucker presents Bruce Nauman's Body art in phenomenological terms:

This concern with physical self is not simple artistic egocentrism, but use of the body to transform intimate subjectivity into objective demonstration. Man is the perceiver and the perceived; he acts and is acted upon; he is the sensor and the sensed. His behavior constitutes a dialectical interchange with the world he occupies. Merleau-Ponty, in *The Structure of Behavior,* stresses that man *is,* in fact, his body. . . . Nauman has used himself in this way as a proto-typical subject for the pieces. These works are meant, essentially, to be encountered privately by one person at a time. Where earlier the artist was the subject and object of recorded situations, now it is the spectator who becomes both the actor and observer of his own activity. [25]

The videos, performance pieces, and body casts by Nauman, to which Tucker is referring, support her reading and are illuminated by her approach. In a broad sense, phenomenology lends itself to approaching installation works. Minimal sculpture—abstract, clean, spare, and part of a controlled situation—is far from the junk aesthetic and spontaneity of the Environments of Oldenburg, Kaprow, and Dine. Yet the critics grappling with those Environments a decade earlier demonstrated that they too, as spectators, had become "the actor and observer" of their own activity. They did not have the same degree of sophistication in their responses, but seem to have instinctually reached similar conclusions.

There are circles of overlapping experience between the Judson artists and the Minimalists. Walter de Maria, for example, had a close association with the Happenings of Robert Whitman and Jim Dine. Dan Flavin had shown at the Judson Gallery in 1961. Robert Morris was involved with dance at Judson. Despite these and other associations, there was a wide range of perception of the art object and the viewer's relationship to it. The following comparison illustrates some differences between artists' notions of spectator participation. In 1961, the year that Kaprow created his labyrinth of chicken wire and newspaper in *An Apple Shrine* at the Judson Gallery, Robert Morris installed *Passageway* in Yoko Ono's studio in New York on Chambers Street (figure 2.6). It was a plywood corridor extending fifty feet and steadily narrowing all the way. As they walked the curving length of the passage, visitors became acutely aware of the gradual compression.

The fine line that Kaprow had walked between manipulating the audience and allowing the audience to participate was more frankly authoritarian in Morris's work. Not everyone liked the experience of *Passageway*. It provoked one visitor, the dancer Yvonne Rainer, to scribble "Fuck You Bob Morris" on one of its walls.[26]

In 1968, Kaprow would publicly take issue with Morris, in his article "How Anti-Form Is Anti-Form?" Recognizing that Morris and some of his contemporaries had concerns akin to those of his own circle of from a few years earlier, Kaprow pointed out that there is a difference between completely filling, even obliterating a space (as he had done at Judson) and placing an object within a space to which it would bear a relationship. In both cases, there has been a shift from the exhibition of autonomous objects to the incorporation of the site of display into the conceptual parameters of art works, but Kaprow did not address this issue. Where the works were created made a significant difference to him:

Morris may not have been in New York during the mid-'50s and early '60s to see the Environments and environmental settings for Happenings, made by Dine, myself, Oldenburg and Whitman. These were akin to his present interests, except that they employed a great variety of media. . . . These Environments tended to fill, and often actually did fill, their entire containing areas, nearly obliterating the ruled definition of the rooms. And although the artists may have had other, more pressing concerns than that of separating their activities from subordination to an architectural enclosure, the thought was in the air and the treatment of those room surfaces was pretty carefree. The important fact was that almost everything was built into the space it was shown in, not transported from studio to showcase.[27]

By the time Kaprow wrote these words, Morris had moved away from the construction of abstract geometric sculpture (which he had not been involved with to the exclusion of other kinds of artistic activity), and was making what came to be known as Process art. But Kaprow's words apply to Minimalism. Minimal sculptures were generally made in a studio or a factory and transported to an exhibition space. Many of the sculptures of Morris, Judd, Andre, and Serra were made out of lasting materials. Morris's large geometric sculptures were made of plywood, and could be taken apart and reconstructed for the next space. Still, an element of the ephemeral was involved in terms of the situation of which the sculptures were originally part. What Kenneth Baker said about the long-term problems of Minimalism resonates for Environments and for later Installation art as well: "The difficulty of writing about Minimalism in retrospect is that it is no longer possible to put most works of the Minimalist period to the test of the experience they promise."[28] Much Minimal sculpture has been preserved and can be put on permanent display; however, this strips something from the works: the opportunity for interaction between the work and the spectator. Baker continues: "The confrontational qualities of all but a few well-known Minimalist works . . . have been irreparably blunted by the works' rapid absorption into the canon of modern art, or at least into the art system. The question of an object's recognizability as art—the question that freshens one's first perception of it—is rendered trivially rhetorical by museums when they display Minimalist works as tokens of a movement and a period."[29] The complex issue of the relationship between situation-based art and museums is further taken up in chapter 3.

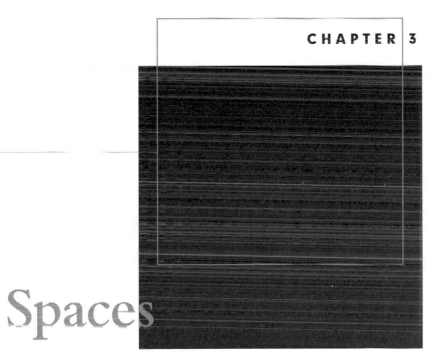

Spaces

Assimilation of the Installation art idea into powerful and prestigious New York museums began at the end of the 1960s, partly as a result of pressure from various artist groups that were forming at the time. For some artists, the temporary nature of Installation art was a gesture of protest at a time when the museum's authority as an institution was being questioned. However, the environmental idea included a rhetoric of inclusion that was appealing to museums. So, inviting artists to create works in situ demonstrated cooperation with groups that were publicly criticizing these institutions.

Creating art that questioned the system through which it would pass was also a gesture of political protest by the end of the 1960s, in part because the museum was seen by many in the art community as the embodiment of political evil. Specifically, the Museum of Modern Art was under fire because of its perceived connection, via its board members, to the Vietnam war. Because of these linkages, questioning the museum became a way of expressing larger political views. Conversely, protesting Vietnam became a way of protesting the museum.

Artist involvement in antiwar activities was on the rise by 1969, but the war was not the only galvanizing force for organizing. As even the briefest chronology of the late 1960s demonstrates, these years saw multiple uprisings and conflicts—not only in the United States, but all over the world. Race riots raged in American cities each summer from 1964 to 1968. The assassinations of Reverend Dr. Martin Luther King, Jr., and Robert Kennedy in 1968 and the police raid at the Stonewall Bar in New York in 1969 that led to the gay liberation movement all acted to further divide parts of American society and unite others, including the artists' community. Widely publicized activities were organized by the Black Emergency Cultural Coalition, the Art Workers' Coalition, the Guerrilla Art Action Group (GAAG), and Women Artists in Revolution (W.A.R.)—groups which all formed in 1969. With the rise of these groups the notion of artists as a political force was renewed—something that had not existed in America in a large sense since the 1930s. This idea represented a redefinition of the arena of art—it now extended into the realm of politics. As Jeanne Siegel voiced in her 1970 interview with Carl Andre: "It seems to be a moment in history when the artist, after twenty-five years of withdrawal, is once again thinking about himself in close relationship to society with the same demands and desires as other human beings."[1] Collectively, the artists tested their power as a political force. American society was split into "hawks" (supporters of the war) and "doves" (opponents of the war). In the art world, this divisiveness was played out between museums and artists. The artists' community overwhelmingly opposed the war, and this shared opposition created a sense of unity for that community.

One of the earliest manifestations of the art world's involvement in the peace movement was Mark Di Suvero's construction of a sixty-foot high tower in Los Angeles in 1966. Far from any museum presence, works by hundreds of participating artists from all across the country were hung on the tower. The project was led by Di Suvero and Irving Petlin. Other protests from the art community also took place outside of the museum context, and in some cases took the form of Installation art. In New York City in October 1967, the Judson Gallery at Judson Memorial Church held a series of twelve events under the collective title *Twelve Evenings of Manipulations*. The series was scheduled to coincide with the march on Washington against the Vietnam war. Although the original Judson artists had long since moved on, the gallery had continued to be involved with the community and to show art. Some of the original Judson artists were invited back to participate in the show, and Allan Kaprow agreed to include his piece *Push and Pull: A Furniture Comedy for Hans Hofmann*. Claes Oldenburg declined the invitation to participate. Of the twelve events in the *Manipulations* series, several of them were Environments. Environments had the potential to break down "elitist" barriers between the visitor and the work of art; they invited participation. The idea of being a social or political activist could include being an active participant in a work of art. Geoff Hendricks made a multimedia Environment for the series called *Sky/Change*. Jean Toche, who would become one of the founding members of the Guerrilla Art Action Group in 1969, here created an Environment entitled *Labyrinths and Psychological Stress*. It involved the participant traversing a narrow base lined with bright floodlights. An alarm was triggered by the motion of walking the length of the piece (figure 3.1). Carolee Schneemann's Environment, *Divisions and Rubble*, invited the viewer to destroy the work. In the program notes she described her piece as follows: "Basic image An environment which people will have to destroy to enter it, to move in it: means of action altering action/means of perception altering perception. An exposed process."[2] Some of the elements in the Environment included a rotten mattress, plastic garbage bags filled with leaves, old clothes, and other debris. Slides flashed, cloth and paper enclosures could be torn away. There was a tape recording of crying cats. Schneemann described the outcome of the piece: Carol Grossberg, then director of Angry Arts Against the War in Vietnam, entered and then destroyed the

3.1
Jean Toche,
*Labyrinths and
Psychological
Stress*, 1967.
Installed at the
Judson Gallery,
New York, during
*Twelve Evenings of
Manipulations.*
Photograph by
Julie Abeles.

Environment, leading the way for other visitors to participate in a similar vein (figure 3.2).

In notes made after the event, organizer Jon Hendricks stated how the works in the series were politically relevant because they presented an antidote to social and political passivity:

Ortiz was relevant. So were all the others—Schneemann's rubble; Bici's ice; Kaprow's room ripped apart; Picard's simple morality play; Goldstein's spliced state of the nation; Geoff's painted-over painting of sky and Toche's blinding lights and Kate Millett's caged people and Steve Rose's enclosed man and Al Hansen's beast man spat upon, and the twelve events ended with Paik cutting his arms with a razor blade while Charlotte Moorman lay on her back playing a cello. The events [the twelve evenings of manipulations] are relevant. It is important that they happened. They are relevant to a state of mind that says

3.2
Carolee Schneemann,
Divisions and Rubble,
1967.
Mixed media.
Installed at the
Judson Gallery,
New York, during
*Twelve Evenings of
Manipulations*.
Carolee Schneemann
on the left.
Photograph by
Charlotte Victoria.

I don't give a shit, it doesn't concern me, I'm removed, I don't want to get involved.

Hendricks referred to the artists who participated as "deconstructionists," and made it clear that creating works of art that would stand outside the commodity system was consistent with their political goals:

[The events] are relevant too to a condition of art that says pure/considered/constructed/classic. The deconstructionists are an opposition; they are a romantic movement. They are messy and aren't very polite. It would be kind of hard to show them at Castelli's this year. Not much to buy, either. Maybe they are anti-American.[3]

Creating a work that could not be commodified was a political gesture aimed at the entire art system, which was increasingly under fire by the artistic community. Hendricks himself, with Jean Toche and Poppy Johnson, formed the Guerrilla Art Action Group in 1969. Acting alone or occasionally in conjunction with members of the Art Workers' Coalition, GAAG staged protests at major New York cultural institutions.

Through the end of the 1960s and into the 1970s, tension grew between artists and museums. This tension was related to both the specific functions of museums and to a perception of their larger political associations. Robert Morris and other artists tested their authority with protests such as the 1970 Art Strike Against Racism, War, and Oppression, in which they demanded that New York City's museums close for the day to show solidarity.[4] The question of where the money that supported the museums was coming from (investments in southeast Asia, for example) was raised by the artists. Gregory Battcock was an articulate spokesperson for the position adopted by many artists:

The trustees of the museums direct NBC and CBS, the *New York Times* and the Associated Press, and that greatest cultural travesty of modern times—The Lincoln Center. They own AT&T, Ford, General Motors, the great multi-billion dollar foundations, Columbia University, Alcoa, Minnesota Mining, United Fruit and AMK, besides sitting on the boards of each others' museums. The implications of these facts are enormous. Do you realize that it is those art-loving, culturally committed trustees of the Metropolitan and Modern museums who are waging the war in Vietnam?[5]

The Rockefellers, who were closely associated with the Museum of Modern Art, became a particular focus for the artists' community. The Rockefellers were seen as politically conservative capitalists who supported as well as profited from the war. The funds they contributed to the Museum of Modern Art—and by extension the institution itself—were perceived by the artists as tainted.

Making art that would stand outside the museum system was one way for artists to express their unwillingness to cooperate with the Rockefellers and their colleagues at other museums. For the most part, the specific political convictions of many artists in the late 1960s and early 1970s did not have the sort of direct visual counterpart in their work that one might expect, given the intensity of the times. Lucy Lippard, in a 1987 essay, recalls the sense she'd had twenty years earlier of "an aesthetic radicalism in the air that might parallel or give form to the political radicalism of the times."[6] But these parallels did not erupt into widespread instances of explicitly political art. It was one thing to issue statements and attend demonstrations. It was quite another to openly infuse art with those same convictions. As Lippard stated later:

Despite the politically charged atmosphere of the late '60s and the sense of hope paradoxically underlying the deathlike surfaces of late Minimalism and the aesthetic denials of much conceptual art, few avant-garde artists found direct ways to reflect their politics in their art. Political naïveté, fear of activism, careerism, lack of support, and a basic incomprehension of how the World really works finally led not to change but back to the artworld, from which bastion artists can remain safely "critical" of society without having to worry about being heard.[7]

But if a specific sociopolitical agenda did not permeate the works of many artists, a general sense of consciousness that society was dividing and unraveling did. As an alternative to the narrative iconography or open propaganda found in socially engaged art of the past, artists developed new forms in which to express their positions. The simple fact of looking for and inventing new forms implies a radical, tradition-breaking stance.

Installation art was only one of the possible ways of accomplishing the goals shared by many in the artists' community; other options included Performance art, Earth art, video art, Process art, and Conceptual art. All of these forms were difficult or even impossible to collect and commodify. By virtue of their ephemeral nature, these forms challenged the market system of the art world and by extension became a protest against the politics of the institutions.

In the 1960s and 1970s, the phrase "painting is dead" was fre-
quently proclaimed as the loss of faith in painting as the essential
embodiment of art was felt throughout the art world. For artists who
wished to be engaged in a living issue, to be painting was to be missing out. Worse, it symbolized compliance with the system. The need
for new forms of art that would retain their integrity was clearly
articulated by the Art Workers' Coalition:

In general, the art object is inadequate to the artist as a means of barter for
the necessities of life, irrelevant to the people in a world of hunger, war and
racial injustice and precious only to the rich who use it to increase their
wealth and maintain their position.

To resolve the conflict, artists must develop art that is real for our time,
and that is meaningful to those not in on the making of it, that reaches the
people and that does not reinforce the horrible sanctity of private property.[8]

Installation art fulfilled some of the same conditions as other transient, noncommodifiable forms. But it also had unique potential for
audience participation. By virtue of the physical involvement it often
demanded of the viewer, Installation art could also change the atmosphere of a museum. That atmosphere was described by painter David
Lee at the open hearing of the Art Workers' Coalition in April 1969:
"Museums, by opening themselves up to the public, are able to edu-
cate non-collectors as to what their personal attitude should be vis-
à-vis the private property of the rich. Namely, DO NOT TOUCH.
Also, don't smoke and keep moving."[9] Installation art had the potential to change the relationship between the viewer and the work of
art, and could break the rules of proper museum decorum.

The 1970 Art Strike Against Racism, War, and Oppression had called upon all the museums in New York City to close for one day to protest the war in Vietnam. But from the beginning, the Museum of Modern Art was singled out for protest by the Art Workers' Coalition because of its immence influence and authority. Spokespeople for the coalition stated, "The reason the AWC chose MoMA as an initial target was not only because it was the establishment of establishments, but because its members were sufficiently concerned with the Museum's functions and its collections to work hard for change."[10] The pressure put on the museum by the Art Workers' Coalition was not without effect. Bates Lowry, who became director of the museum in 1968, promised the Art Workers' Coalition that he would form a Committee on Artists' Relations in which artists could participate.[11] Some of his aims for the institution paralleled those of the coalition. For example, shortly after his appointment as director was announced, he had spoken out on the need for the Museum of Modern Art to exhibit current art in a more timely fashion. Unfortunately, he was forced to resign in May of 1969 after less than a year in office. There was speculation in the press that his desire to make many changes was one reason.[12] Lowry's successor, John Hightower, also had an unusually short tenure. His interest in engaging the museum with social and political issues, and his support of contemporary artists, was seen as incompatible with the museum's aims, so he was asked to resign early in 1972.[13]

The Art Workers' Coalition made demands specific to the Museum of Modern Art's function as a museum, including a wing devoted to the art of African-American and Puerto Rican artists, and inclusion of artists on the board of trustees. They also criticized the amount of resources spent on the permanent collection, demanding instead that more space be given to one-man exhibitions of contemporary art. The coalition tried to redefine the museum in more populist terms, demanding more community outreach. Early in 1970, after months of pressure from the Art Workers' Coalition, the Museum of Modern Art (where the admission price at the time was $1.50) instituted a free day on Mondays. Although the free day was subsequently discontinued, it did represent an attempt to make the museum available to a wider segment of the population. By the fall of 1968, the museum began to show works that had the capacity to reach out and engage the public, turning viewers into participants.

Robert Rauschenberg's installation, entitled *Soundings,* was shown at the Museum of Modern Art in the fall of 1968. *Soundings* was made by Rauschenberg for an exhibition at the Stedelijk Museum in Amsterdam. It was an installation with a high degree of audience participation. Along one wall in a darkened room, layers of plexiglass panels were electronically activated by the voice and other sounds made by the viewer upon entering—images of chairs would flash across the panels when stimulated by sound. Without the sounds created by the visitors, the piece appeared as a wall of dim mirrored surfaces (figure 3.3).[14] The Museum of Modern Art's press release read: "Rauschenberg's requirement that the viewer participate in the creation of the work of art is a radical departure from the traditional relation between artist and audience. . . . In *Soundings,* he insists that the viewer become his collaborator; without him the work does not exist."[15] The museum presented the exhibition with viewer participation as its selling point, indicating the value the institution placed on this aspect at the time. Full-scale installations were not shown at the museum until 1969—eleven years after Kaprow's first Environment. In fact, installations of any kind came late to this institution, and by the time they came, it was in a Minimal-Conceptual context.

The entry of installations into museums in New York coincided with the beginning of the institutionalization of Process art. There was an overlap between Process art, Conceptual art, and installations in terms of their challenge to museum practice. The overlap stemmed from a shared value placed by some of the artists on ephemerality and thus resistance to preservation and collection. Artists engaged in Process art often used perishable materials such as ice, mist, or sawdust. These were not simply throwaway materials, but ones that would, over time, cease to exist: melting, evaporating, or being swept away. Perhaps most challenging, from an institutional perspective, was the fact that Conceptual, Process, and installation works usually could not be seen by curators before they were installed, but were created

3.3
Robert
Rauschenberg,
Soundings, 1968.
Installation view of
the exhibition *Robert
Rauschenberg:
Soundings*. Museum
of Modern Art, New
York. 22 October
1968 through 26
January 1969.
Photograph © 1999
The Museum of
Modern Art,
New York.

by the artist, in situ, shortly before the exhibitions opened to the public.

In the spring of 1969, shortly after hiring two young new associate curators, Marcia Tucker and James Monte, the Whitney Museum of American Art presented *Anti-Illusion: Procedures/Materials,* an exhibition of Process art that included scatter pieces, video and extended time pieces, and concert performances. The exhibition was curated by Tucker and Monte and included works by twenty-one artists, among them Robert Morris, Michael Asher, Bruce Nauman, Keith Sonnier, Carl Andre, Barry Le Va, Robert Ryman, Richard Serra, Joel Shapiro, Eva Hesse, Rafael Ferrer, and Lynda Benglis. There were also related video and film performances that were presented over the course of a week, including concerts by Steve Reich and Philip Glass.[16] For the most part, the pieces were constructed within the museum itself, and were dismantled at the close of the exhibition. There were several works, however, including Hesse's resin piece, *Expanded Expansion,* that were portable and more permanent.

The catalog to the exhibition contains essays by Monte and Tucker, and a bibliography that includes both Wittgenstein's *Philosophical Investigations* and Merleau-Ponty's *Phenomenology of Perception,* asserting the importance of these works for understanding the new art. Monte's introductory words in the catalog acknowledge the ways in which organizing *Anti-Illusion: Procedures/Materials* departed from traditional ways of curating an exhibition:

During its organization, we discovered that the normal curatorial procedures of seeing and then selecting or rejecting works to be included could not be followed. After visiting numerous studios and galleries, as well as viewing slides and photographs, we discovered that the bulk of the exhibition would be comprised of painting and sculpture which we had not seen and would not see until perhaps one week before the opening date of the show. That this method of putting together an exhibition is risky for the artist as well as the Museum goes without saying.[17]

The risk was met with a fairly unenthusiastic critical reception. Rafael Ferrer's two works were singled out for criticism by both Peter Schjeldahl and Hilton Kramer, the former finding them the "most outrageous" in the show.[18] One of Ferrer's works, *Ice*, consisted of ice blocks on the ramp leading up to the front door of the museum; the piece melted after seventy-three hours. Ferrer's other work in the exhibition was called *Hay, Grease, Steel* and consisted of a pile of hay, a grease smeared wall to which more hay was stuck, and steel weights. The ephemerality of many of the works in the exhibition was found to be problematic by both Schjeldahl and Kramer—not because they wanted the works to stick around, but because it violated their sense of what an art object is. Emily Wasserman, reviewing the exhibition for *Artforum*, felt that too many artists were included, causing disorganization and too broad a view. But she also praised the Whitney, saying, "That its new curators were able to coordinate. . . an exhibition which was relevant to the most current preoccupations of a considerable group of artists, is credit to a boldness and awareness beyond mere trend-following."[19]

The works in *Anti-Illusion* engaged the spectator in a variety of ways, indicating the continuation of the importance of viewer engagement in Process art. Bruce Nauman's corridor piece, entitled *Performance Area,* was Environment-like in that it allowed the viewer to enter and traverse a space. This work, like his other corridor pieces, was participatory in an individual, behaviorist way that engaged the spectator in a role controlled by the absent artist, who nonetheless was present, in a sense, through the control he exerted (figure 3.4). The corridor was extremely narrow, and as with Nauman's other corridors, the effect on the spectator was often uneasiness. As Peter Schjeldahl later wrote of Nauman's corridor pieces overall:

Nauman ran into definite trouble with New York audiences when he started showing austere, "behaviorist" environments—a corridor so narrow it could be passed through only sideways, a suspended "room" whose walls stopped at mid-shin level—that induced physical self-consciousness and mild sensory deprivation. Nervous urbanites (including me) found such work conducive less to mind expansion than to anxiety attack.[20]

3.4
Installation view of the exhibition *Anti-Illusion: Procedures/Materials*. Bruce Nauman's *Performance Area* is visible against the far wall. Whitney Museum of American Art, New York. 19 May through 6 July 1969. Photography © Estate of Peter Moore, New York.

Barry Le Va's piece in *Anti-Illusion* was participatory in a more subtle way. A California artist exhibiting in New York for the first time in this exhibition, Le Va covered a section of the floor of the museum with a fine layer of flour in an irregular shape. Although viewers did not walk on it directly, the piece still changed constantly from the movement of people in the gallery. As Marcia Tucker later wrote about Le Va, "it is the viewer who must provide, in all of Le Va's work, the information which is absent in the physical aspects of each piece. . . . The properties of the phenomena being observed will change according to the activities of the observer"[21] (figure 3.5).

A year after *Anti-Illusion: Procedures/Materials*, the Jewish Museum mounted the exhibition *Using Walls*, curated by Susan T. Goodman, then assistant curator. *Using Walls* had an outdoor as well as an indoor component, with the outdoor component spread around

3-5
Barry Le Va,
*Extended Vertex
Meetings: Blocked,
Blown Outwards, #1*,
1969–1971. Blown
flour. Approximately
25 x 85 feet.
Courtesy Danese,
New York.

the city in the form of painting on the exteriors of buildings. The indoor component consisted of works made by artists directly on the museum's walls. Sol LeWitt, Daniel Buren, Mel Bochner, and Lawrence Weiner were among the artists who participated. LeWitt executed a wall drawing for the exhibition. He had established a basis for his work in his 1967 statement: "I will refer to the kind of art in which I am involved as conceptual art. In conceptual art the idea or concept is the most important aspect of the work . . . all planning and decisions are made beforehand and the execution is a perfunctory affair. The idea becomes the machine that makes the art." [22] LeWitt's wall drawings were executed directly on the wall, but they can still be collected. The owner receives a certificate on which is a photo of the work and written instructions. The owner is then authorized to execute the wall drawing.

Like the Whitney's *Anti-Illusion* exhibition, the works in *Using Walls* were not seen by the museum staff until they were in progress or completely installed. The Jewish Museum had a unique position among New York museums, functioning with the freedom and daring of an alternative space, so the entry of ephemeral art into its galleries did not constitute the same kind of conflict between the radical and the establishment as it did at the Museum of Modern Art or even at the Whitney. *Using Walls* was an important early instance of artists creating works directly in a museum situation, and the artists in *Using Walls* were given plenty of leeway in creating their pieces (for example, Lawrence Weiner was allowed to cut away a chunk of wall in one gallery). Nineteen-seventy was also the year of *Information,* the landmark exhibition of Conceptual art at the Museum of Modern Art, curated by Kynaston McShine, who had left the Jewish Museum for MoMA in 1968. This show contained a selection of material produced by artists from all over the world, and much of it pertained to the Vietnam war.

The first exhibition at the Museum of Modern Art of what can properly be called Installation art was *Spaces,* held from 30 December 1969 through 1 March 1970. Because this show was specifically dedicated to the exhibition of installations, it warrants close analysis. Conceived and organized by associate curator Jennifer Licht, the exhibition included installations by five individual artists and one group: Michael Asher, Larry Bell, Dan Flavin, Robert Morris, Pulsa (a group consisting of, at the time, Michael Cain, Patrick Clancy, William Crosby, William Duesing, Paul Fuge, Peter Kindlmann, and David Rumsey), and Franz Erhard Walther. This was the first time that artists were invited by the Museum of Modern Art to create works in situ at the museum rather than creating them in the studio where they could be seen and selected beforehand by a curator. *Spaces* opened six months after the Whitney had shown *Anti-Illusion,* and some of the same artists were included in both exhibitions. The idea for *Spaces* was first presented to the staff in May 1969, and the show was speedily organized. One reason for doing the exhibition was pressure from artists. From Licht's later comments regarding *Spaces,* it becomes clear how, from an institutional point of view, allowing artists to build ephemeral works within the walls of the museum was a concession to political pressure. In Licht's words:

This was a period when many pressure groups, representing various constituencies, were active. (The Art Workers' Coalition, which was a powerful lobby, had . . . already been formed.) Pressure from vocal sources in the art community was probably a significant factor in enabling me to achieve an exhibition that departed from traditional practices at MOMA and was artist-oriented.[23]

As Licht wrote in a memo to Walter Bareiss, then director of operations: "The exhibition will really be a test of the flexibility of our working systems, and will need a strong communal effort from everyone to succeed."[24] From the memos that remain, this appears to have been an understatement. The museum staff had to contend with such things as ordering thousands of pairs of paper slippers for visitors to don and shopping bags in which to carry their shoes. (Eventually the museum gave up on both these niceties and visitors were asked to simply remove their shoes and carry them.) Other issues included safety problems, posed by visitors having to navigate darkened rooms, and general maintenance problems.

In the planning stages, the exhibition was called *Environments*. The eventual choice of the title *Spaces* was related to space exploration—1969 was the year that United States astronaut Neil Armstrong became the first man to walk on the moon. The cover of the *Spaces* catalog shows a dark sky studded with stars and planets.

In *Spaces,* the artists treated a space large enough for the viewer to enter as a single work, rather than as a gallery to be filled with discrete objects. Emphasis was placed on the experience the viewer would have. The works included in *Spaces* were installed directly in the galleries, tailored to the configurations of the spaces they occupied, and were dismantled following the exhibition. The museum was committed to giving free rein to the artists, and regarding restrictions, the catalog acknowledges only one: Robert Morris's piece consisted of miniature groves of Norway spruce trees planted in diminishing size. In order to maintain a plant-friendly climate, special humidity and temperature conditions had to be maintained. The catalog notes how "originally the air was to be imbued with an additional fillip, negative ions, which induce feelings of euphoria, but this aspect could not be realized."[25] If there were other restrictions, always a question with commissioned works, no record of them is available. Licht's letters of invitation to the artists specified only that "the concept is the employment of a cohesive spatial situation in a single work."[26] In her letter to Franz Erhard Walther, Licht said: "About 8 artists will be invited to create a work of their choice, each in a room under his control. Is the idea of a work that exists for and uses a specific room or area of interest to you? There will be no stylistic theme or grouping, and the other artists might include, for example, Morris and Flavin with the kind of environmental work they have made for a special room or gallery."[27] Thus, site specificity was very important. In fact, it was the defining characteristic of the work Licht envisioned for the show, rather than spectator participation. Interestingly, Walther's piece, *Instruments for Processes*, incorporated the presence of the artist. It was Walther's idea that he and/or his wife be present, and when they were not there, that viewers not be permitted to enter the space (figure 3.6). The press release announced. "Under the supervision of the artist, visitors are invited to participate in the use of his 'instruments for processes.' . . . The artist and his wife will be present at stated hours to assist."[28] The installation had canvas covering the floor, with visitors able to put on, climb into, and pick up canvas, felt, and leather objects Walther had made for the space, including climbing into canvas bags that had pockets for five people. During the

3.6
Franz Erhard Walther,
*Instruments for
Processes*, 1969.
Installation view of
the exhibition
Spaces. Museum of
Modern Art, New
York. 30 December
1969 through
1 March 1970.
Photograph © 1999
The Museum of
Modern Art,
New York.

3.7
Franz Erhard
Walther, schedule
for *Instruments for
Processes*, 1969.
From the *Spaces*
exhibition. Museum
of Modern Art, New
York. 30 December
1969 through
1 March 1970.
Photograph © 1999
The Museum of
Modern Art,
New York.

Franz Erhard Walther
will be present
at the times indicated below
to use his pieces with the public

January

S	M	T	W	T	F	S
				1	2	3
4	5	6	7	8	9	10
11	12	13	14	15	16	17
18	19	20	21	22	23	24
25	26	27	28	29	30	31

11 a.m. to 1 p.m.
Noon to 2 p.m.
3 p.m. to 5 p.m.
7 p.m. to 9 p.m.

hours when the artist was not present, visitors could only look into the room, but not enter or use anything (figure 3.7). Walther had written to Licht before the exhibition opened: "It is necessary to show the use of the objects to the public. That could be done for two hours on each day. . . . During the remaining hours the objects are just exposed along with informations and explanations about the use/employment of things. . . . For certain reasons I want to show and explain the function of the things by myself."[29] Even when Walther was present, one could not just walk in: in order to avoid having the space become too crowded, the artist invited people in at his discretion. In this piece, participation was only under the explicit direction and supervision of the artist, who controlled the action.

Although the other five works did not rely on the presence of the artist or specific activities for the spectator/participant, the presence of the viewer and an interaction between the viewer and the piece was certainly intended to be a factor. Michael Asher used his space to create a room lined on the ceiling, walls, and floor with acoustic paneling (figure 3.8). The environment absorbed ambient sounds, in some areas more than others. In the corners of the room, sound was almost totally absorbed, creating near total silence. Asher even placed the constructed wall sections on rubber pads to eliminate vibrations. To protect the fiberglass floor, visitors were not permitted to wear shoes in the space, but once inside, they were permitted to relax on the floor, and to stay as long as they liked. In addition to the practical necessity of protecting the floor, removing shoes before entering the work also literally meant leaving the grit of the street behind. Asher's piece was not intended to merge with or seem continuous with the outside environment. Its floor-to-ceiling walls

isolated it not only from the street outside, but from the rest of the museum as well.[30]

Larry Bell's room was completely darkened, with black walls and floor, and divided by a partition. Coated sheets of glass reflected streaks of light, which came from an exterior source reflected from a white wall outside the room. Viewers had to navigate their way through the darkened space. In Dan Flavin's *Untitled (For Sonja),* two opposing wall-length rows of fluorescent lights were presented, one low, one high, one green, one yellow, creating a light filled environment (figure 3.9). Robert Morris created a room in which the viewer had to stand constricted in a narrow, shoulder-high, cruciform trench. Looking up, one could see four groves of live spruce trees, planted in descending size. The trees sloped upward toward the corners of the room, and provided a false sense of spatial recession. A fine mist filled the room (figure 3.10). Pulsa used the sculpture garden to set up an elaborate system of lights and sounds that responded to ambient stimuli, although not with the one-to-one directness of Rauschenberg's *Soundings.*

Licht, a young associate curator from England, presented her idea for the exhibition to the other members of the Museum of Modern Art staff using the following arguments:

Recent manifestations of art move away from the creation of an enduring object which maintains its own presence spatially and physically. The artists concerned are altering or discarding the traditional dichotomy of viewer and static object for an environmental situation, which envelops and enmeshes the viewer in a fuller involvement with actual space and a more mandatory interaction with the art. . . .

Certainly a conscious issue of the current preoccupation with enormous physiographical artworks is the unfeasibility of subjecting this art to the usual processes through which the traditional art object—controllable, containable, portable, preservable and hence marketable—is passed.[31]

She urged the museum to be responsive to the nontraditional aspects of the newest art and to accept the challenge that such work presented. In her final statement, she called on the museum's to be an institution at the service of the public, stressing that whereas a commercial gallery whose existence depends on works that are marketable could not show ephemeral work, the museum could: "Some of the aims of the recent artists' protests have been directed toward disassociating art

3.9
Dan Flavin, *Untitled (For Sonja)*, 1969. Installation view of the exhibition *Spaces*. Museum of Modern Art, New York. 30 December 1969 through 1 March 1970. Photograph © 1999 The Museum of Modern Art, New York.

from the marketing system, and demands were made of museums to accept some direct responsibility. The works for this exhibition will be created especially, and dismantled afterwards. Here we can assume a role that belongs uniquely to the public institution and lies outside the domain of the art dealer."[32] Licht appears to have been striving to find a role for the museum that was outside the market system.

Although Licht's internal memo acknowledged that the kind of work in *Spaces* questioned the structure of the art world's marketing system, none of the materials generated by the museum for public consumption mentioned those issues. Instead, it was the notion of the spectator as participant that the museum played up in presenting the show to the public. The press release stated: "Actual space is now

3.10
Robert Morris, *Untitled.* Installation view of the exhibition *Spaces.* Museum of Modern Art, New York. 30 December 1969 through 1 March 1970. Photograph © 1999 The Museum of Modern Art, New York.

being employed as an active ingredient, and the scope of the work of art has expanded to include the viewer." It was a novelty to be able to enter a work of art: "In this exhibition you don't observe what the artist has done, you experience it. You actually go into the work of art."[33] This idea was also emphasized in Licht's catalog essay:

[Space] is now being considered as an active ingredient, not simply to be represented but to be shaped and characterized by the artist, and capable of involving and merging the viewer and art in a situation of greater scope and scale. In effect, one now enters the interior space of the work of art . . . and is presented with a set of conditions rather than a finite object. Working within the almost unlimited potential of these enlarged, more spatially complex circumstances, the artist is now free to influence and determine, even govern, the sensations of the viewer. The human presence and perception of the spatial context have become materials of art.[34]

Licht's remarks have an interesting relationship with the discussions of phenomenology that were beginning to gain currency. She expressed the idea of the work of art as a set of conditions established by the artist to be experienced by the viewer.

It is interesting to see the effect on Installation art of larger spaces, more money, and more elaborate materials—and particularly of sophisticated technology. These were all available, in nearly unprecedented amounts, to the artists participating in *Spaces* as a result of substantial corporate support for the exhibition; and some of the installations were technically elaborate and quite expensive. This magnitude drew attention to the patronage factor, reflecting a spirit of acquiescence rather than rebellion. Dan Flavin, who received donations of materials for his piece from General Electric, was criticized by the Art Workers' Coalition for this concession, and urged to drop out of the exhibition.[35] Collaboration with the museum was clearly not automatic or necessarily enviable at this time. Gregory Battcock, writing about the exhibition for *Arts* magazine, picked up on this issue, but he exonerated the artists and blamed the museum. His article, entitled "The Politics of Space," focused on the morally questionable coupling of corporate funds and the Museum of Modern Art:

It's too bad that nobody noticed that many of the contributors to the show (or their parent companies) engage in research and production activities that, either directly or indirectly, have benefited the Department of Defense and American genocide in Vietnam. . . .

The artists get their materials where they can. Why not? There is no connection that can be philosophically demonstrated between the art works themselves and the war. However there is just one connection. . . . The Museum sets itself up as a guardian and contributor to the culture. . . . And what is the museum doing about its involvement with art? It didn't even bother to check up on the firms they solicited equipment from. They have helped the corporate mentalities to ease their burden of guilt and, having said their five Hail Marys, their conscience.[36]

Despite the unconventional nature of the *Spaces* exhibition, and the Museum of Modern Art's attempts to accommodate artists' demands, James Turrell declined the invitation to participate in the exhibition on principle, because of what museums represented.[37]

The critical response to *Spaces* was mixed. Predictably, it was not taken entirely seriously by some reporters, who described it as if it were a funhouse. As foreshadowed in the criticism of the Environments a decade earlier, the physical experience was singled out: "Before anyone can enter the exhibition, to protect the works he must remove his shoes, don a pair of clumsy paper slippers and then slide along the floors of the show."[38] Nonetheless, the issue of spectator participation was still shown to be of importance, perhaps because it was in these terms that the exhibition was presented. Carter Ratcliff judged the works in *Spaces* on the basis of their success in this regard:

Now—these works in the *Spaces* show are very different. The viewer must enter into them physically. Participation is automatic, denied to no one. The artist can count on a response. His art is in designing an environment where this is the case. His design must be left incomplete. It must, in fact, be a near void or chaos, differentiated or given form only insofar as that form is open— *automatically*—to anyone who enters. Further, this random entering must— *automatically*—result as less formlessness. The participant must feel that his entrance means something, has an effect.[39]

Ratcliff concludes: "Of these four exhibits, Pulsa's is the least successful as an environment. Literally speaking, it is an environment, the most extensive and the most attractive. But the viewer doesn't become a participant."[40] Although viewer participation was the criterion for judging the success of an environment, Ratcliff was not searching for specific activities. An effective environment required something far less tangible: the sense that the viewer was needed to complete the work. Judging from Ratcliff's reaction, it would appear that Pulsa's piece failed as theater, and (in a reverse of Fried's position) this was seen by Ratcliff as problematic.

For the museum, viewer participation had a slightly different resonance. Robert Storr, who became curator of contemporary art at the Museum of Modern Art in 1990, had this to say about the *Spaces* exhibition and the emphasis that was placed on viewer participation:

So little attention is paid to how visitors experience art in museums that the few occasions where you have something that is "interactive," you make the most of it. [*Spaces*] was done in and around the time of relevance and outreach, and basically was the last, that is prior to recently, the last episode of trying to make modern art a populist phenomenon. So I think the ideological context of that is this other factor, and how directly [Licht] or [the museum] thought about the connection, I nonetheless think that it exists in that framework.[41]

In *Spaces* there was an attempt to make the museum experience a more relaxed one. The guards were given special instructions to allow people to sit or lie on the floor and to stay in any of the rooms as long as they wished.[42] For many visitors, the experience of lying barefoot on the floor of the Museum of Modern Art probably did go a long way toward making the place seem more accessible. There was a particular status to the art museum in the United States at the end of the 1960s, and it explains some of the activities at the Museum of Modern Art. Art was to be for everyone, and the museum, as a public institution, would make that possible. During the 1960s, many new museums opened throughout the United States, making art even more accessible, while providing a new source of civic pride. There was a desire to make culture more democratic. It appeared as though not even the Museum of Modern Art—long regarded as a bastion of elitism—was immune to the times, and the *Spaces* exhibition must be seen in this context. It was this populist aspect of the museum that Licht drew on when she pitched her show to the museum staff on the basis of what the museum could do as a public institution.

The Museum of Modern Art found itself in a new role in another sense: Grace Glueck, reviewing *Spaces* for the *New York Times,* acknowledged the new role that the museum was playing:

In effect, the show, whose installations are temporary, adds to the museum's traditional pursuits of collecting, curating and exhibiting, the somewhat radical function as [sic] aesthetic laboratory. And Mrs. Licht, aware that museums and their interest in the "dead" past are increasingly called into question by younger artists, affirms that one of the show's primary purposes is to find out if a museum can be used as a situation for "live" experiments. . . . "I decided to ask for proposals that would make unaccustomed demands on our staff and resources. So, in effect, we became responsible not only for exhibiting the artists' works, but for executing them."[43]

This last quote from Licht about the demanding role of the curator when organizing an exhibition of Installation art indicates the new role of the museum.

Despite the lukewarm critical responses, the *Spaces* exhibition was important for the museum. As Licht stated in retrospect: "*Spaces* . . . received a good deal of corporate financial support, it attracted a lot of press attention, it had a decent audience, and it reduced some of the pressure from the artistic community. By those standards it would be counted a success."[44]

Licht later described the fundamental leap of faith that an exhibition of Installation art entailed. Her remarks, which partially echo those made by James Monte regarding *Anti-Illusion: Procedures/Materials,* summarize the ways in which Installation art first challenged and then altered, at least temporarily, museum practice:

The Museum was a bureaucracy: scores of people were drawn into the process of planning a major exhibition, and many of them knew little about contemporary art. Part of the curatorial devoir is to persuade any number of departments or committees that an idea has validity. Usually this persuasion is based primarily on the presentation of visual material, i.e. photographs of works that will comprise the exhibition. In this case, of course, I did not necessarily know long beforehand exactly what each participant intended to do: indeed, nor did the participant himself always know! At many stages of the planning process, therefore, I was asking people to suspend familiar means of judgement. This naturally provoked philosophical difficulties because the balance of power was changed: authority was rescinded from the institution and devolved instead on the artist.[45]

Although the changes Licht described were true for *Spaces,* they did not represent a permanent change in the way the institution operated. For many years, *Spaces* remained something of an isolated occurrence, despite its success from the museum's point of view. Its most concrete legacy was the Projects series, established in 1971. Proposed by Licht, the Projects series was a direct outgrowth of *Spaces*—continuing the notion of the museum as aesthetic laboratory. With the inauguration of this series, there would always be a space dedicated to new, experimental work in the museum. As Licht later said:

"Certainly *Spaces* helped open the Museum doors for new forms of art, and it furthered freedom of access to artists. Programmes such as Projects, where small galleries were given over to site-specific work . . . followed."[46] The first Projects series ran from 1971 until 1982. Proportionally, the vast majority of exhibitions of contemporary art held at the museum during these years were Projects exhibitions. These shows were not all installations, but some were, and Projects was, for a long time, the main forum within the museum in which anything installation-like was presented. The Projects series guaranteed that the museum would always have something contemporary on view, regardless of its other exhibitions. In the 1970s there were often two or more projects on view simultaneously, in different parts of the museum.

The Projects series was inaugurated with a work by Keith Sonnier, significantly an installation that contained a strong element of spectator participation. Sonnier's installation consisted of a sound and light environment where images of the viewers were projected from one room to another. Video as an art medium was exploited by a number of artists in the 1970s for its potential for involving the spectator.[47] The press release presented the exhibition in what was already becoming familiar language: "In involving the spectator as performer, the changing situation becomes completely different than that of the usual activity in a museum of just looking at objects. . . . The piece is activated through the participation of the visiting public and tries to engage the spectator on a more basic level than just visual perception."[48] The language used here is very similar to that in the press release for Rauschenberg's *Soundings* and also for *Spaces*.

Although only sporadically on view, participatory exhibitions had become established at the museum.

Direct viewer participation in terms of activities appeared again in an exhibition at the Museum of Modern Art with a 1976 Projects show by William T. Wiley. The project, which ran from April 9 through May 16, was designed to encourage activity by the viewer, according to the press release: "While appreciating the need for restrictions, Wiley says he has always understood the urge to touch in museums, and his current installation encourages viewer participation. . . . Museum visitors are invited to play a guitar, throw the *I-Ching,* and look through the notebook Wiley kept while creating the piece."[49] Viewers were also invited to draw with pens on a large plywood heart on the wall, and pastels were reportedly made available for visitors to draw directly on the wall (figure 3.11). The artist was not present.

3.11
Installation view of the exhibition, *Projects: William T. Wiley,* Museum of Modern Art, New York. 2 April through 16 May 1976. Photograph © 1999 The Museum of Modern Art, New York.

Some of the most significant installations shown in major New York art museums during the 1970s contained an explicit institutional critique. Maurice Berger points out that museums changed (as much as they did) partly because some of the artists most critical of the institutions were willing to exhibit in them.[50] But once inside the museum's doors, the most subversive works could be subject to a tame interpretation by the institution, which would affect the way they were understood by the public. Berger observes astutely that with Robert Morris's piece in *Spaces*:

Licht chose to ignore the institutional and ecological implications of Morris's environment. Its rejection of the "inert matter of art" challenges the museum's social hermeticism: The environment was disturbing to many visitors who envisioned in it an inevitable and desolate future. The allusions to landscape painting and states of euphoria were ironic inversions of the work's ultimate appeal to ecological responsibility: Could political and cultural indifference to the consequences of wastefulness and over production result in a world so barren of life-sustaining resources that such resources must be synthesized in order to survive?[51]

Hans Haacke is also well known for questioning the system in which he exhibits, and his *MOMA POLL,* which was shown in the *Information* exhibition at the Museum of Modern Art in 1970, is a prime example of this. Visitors were asked to vote on the question: "Would the fact that Governor Rockefeller has not yet denounced President Nixon's Indochina policy be a reason for you not to vote for him in November?" Two ballot boxes were provided. Approximately twelve percent of the visitors to the exhibition voted, with a majority indicating an affirmative answer. Given the long-standing involvement between the Rockefeller family and the Museum of Modern Art, this question created a clear link between the museum and the current political situation. Viewers could become active participants by deciding to cast a vote.

Although the Museum of Modern Art went on from *Spaces* to *Information* to the Projects series, more than twenty years would pass before the museum again allowed artists to use the museum on a large scale as an "aesthetic laboratory." This lack of sustained commitment to aesthetically and, by extension, socially radical art occurred in other museums that had made a promising start as well. In the fall of 1976, Whitney Museum director Tom Armstrong dismissed Marcia Tucker, citing the desire to focus more on the museum's permanent collection.[52] In the space of a year, site-specific, ephemeral works that the viewer could enter had slipped inside some of the most hallowed museum doors. Initially, the museums may have considered these exhibitions successful on certain levels; however, the problems from the museum perspective began to make themselves known about a year later.

One of the first signs that all was not well was Robert Morris's ill-fated 1971 exhibition at the Tate Gallery in London, where visitors were encouraged to remove their shoes and jump and climb on the structures he had provided. The Tate Gallery shut the exhibition down after only five days claiming concern for the safety of the viewers.[53] Because museums were vulnerable to potential lawsuits, and easily frightened by the potential for disorderly conduct by visitors, participatory environments were to be curtailed.

The safety and efficacy of participatory environments were not the only issues called into question by museums in the early seventies. Philosophical questions about whether certain types of work belonged in a museum were also being raised by the same institutions that had initially opened their doors to many of them. This point was raised by Sir Norman Reid, then director of the Tate, in 1971, following the closing of the Morris exhibition:

An increasing amount of art is being made outside the familiar format of easel painting and studio sculpture and we have to ask ourselves whether the idea of a museum in a traditional sense is compatible with the new activities, spectacles, happenings, earth sculpture and the like which leave no record other than on tape or film. Many artists have declared that they are not interested in the survival of their work and almost with deliberation choose materials which are impermanent. (Incidentally, it may well be regarded as a duty of the permanent collection to acquire such works if only because the works so protected and cared for may be the only examples of their kind which survive.) [54]

The experiments were not seen by the museums as successful, and the museums retreated somewhat. William Rubin, director of painting and sculpture at the Museum of Modern Art, expressed the thought that the museum concept could not expand to accommodate all forms.[55] But if the museum concept seemed finite to Rubin, the art market, by contrast, proved itself quite adaptable. This adaptation, more than anything else, guaranteed that the museum would eventually find a way to accommodate the new forms. Nonetheless, the next part of the story finds Installation art in New York on the margin once again.

CHAPTER 4

Installations

Despite the overtures made by the Museum of Modern Art, the Jewish Museum, and the Whitney Museum at the end of the 1960s, there continued to be a need for alternative exhibition spaces. Some artists forsook all indoor spaces, alternative or otherwise, and instead concentrated on making large-scale Earthworks in geographically remote areas. Michael Heizer's *Double Negative,* 1969 (figure 4.1), is situated in the Nevada desert, and Robert Smithson's *Spiral Jetty,* 1970, is in the Great Salt Lake in Utah. On the other hand, particularly in the early 1970s, there was a burst of installation-type activity in alternative spaces in New York. During this time, the parameters of Installation art were expanded as these installations tried, in new ways, to break down the traditional barrier between the spectator and the work of art. Moreover, in the alternative spaces the characteristics

4.1
Michael Heizer, *Double Negative,* 1969. 240,000-ton displacement in rhyolite and sandstone. 1,500 x 50 x 30 feet. Mormon Mesa, Overton, Nevada. Collection of The Museum of Contemporary Art, Los Angeles.

of the physical space were often integrated into the artworks. This integration allowed viewers to be keenly aware of their surroundings—the art did not exist in a space and time that was separate from theirs.

The two phenomena— installations and alternative spaces—blossomed simultaneously. As Patrick Ireland observed:

The installation idea began again as far as I know in alternative spaces, because the Minimal venture was an impetus to that, because people were doing big things and they were doing stuff that in some ways didn't need a gallery. And then there were a variety of needs that involved abusing the space. . . . And there was a tremendous surge out of the gallery that had to do with an impatience and exhaustion with the confines of the gallery and the lack of permissions within it. And the gallery as a commercial site was rejected in a variety of ways and that led to the installation idea that we know. And I think it paralleled the growth of unofficial institutions.[1]

Alternatives were sought and they were found or created. The years immediately following 1969 were quite active in terms of finding and establishing new exhibition contexts in New York.

Most of the alternative spaces that opened in the early 1970s in New York were in SoHo, where a few commercial galleries had begun to establish themselves at the end of the previous decade. The Paula Cooper Gallery and the Leo Castelli Gallery were among the first, with John Weber, who had previously directed the Martha Jackson Gallery and the Dwan Gallery, opening his gallery in 1971. At some of the galleries, there were possibilities for site specific installations. (For example, Weber had important early exhibitions of

LeWitt's wall drawings.) But there was a greater concentration of exhibitions that incorporated the display site itself at the alternative spaces.

A partial list of the alternative spaces that opened in New York in the early 1970s includes 112 Greene Street in 1971; The Institute for Art and Urban Resources in 1972; the Clocktower and Artists Space in 1973; and P.S. 1 in 1976. The alternative spaces eventually became established in their own right, losing some of their radical status in the process. As Phil Patton observed in 1977, "For all their improvisational character, however, many of these alternative spaces have by now become so firmly a part of the art scene that numerous artists have successfully pursued careers in them alone. If present trajectories of prestige continue, it may soon be as important for a young artist to have a show at a place like P. S. 1 as to become associated with a reputable gallery." [2] It was quite prescient of Patton to have written those words only a few years after such places had opened. But initially, those spaces were underrecognized and shared audiences drawn in large part from the artistic community rather than a larger art-viewing public.

Alternative spaces were not in the business of selling art and because they did not have permanent collections, they could be free of the weight of art history. They could also provide a physical alternative to the pristine conditions of a museum or gallery space. A decade earlier, Kaprow, Oldenburg, and Dine had found the run-down condition of the downtown spaces in which their work was shown to be a contributing rather than detracting factor. Likewise, many of the artists creating installations in New York in the 1970s found something desirable in raw, unfinished spaces like 112 Greene

Street and P.S. 1. The works created in such places responded to the quirks and characters of the exhibition spaces. Indeed, the works seemed to go with the spaces. In response to the opening of P.S. 1, which was an old school building, Nancy Foote commented on the appropriateness of the space in relation to the work shown there: "One can hardly imagine surroundings more potentially hostile to art, but as the Clocktower and 112 Greene Street (which, by comparison, look like MOMA and the Louvre) have proven time and again, this need not be the case."[3]

Some of the reasons for the appeal of these spaces have been articulated most clearly by the artists working in them. Alice Aycock, whose large-scale constructions of the 1970s often allowed for climbing by viewers, later said of 112 Greene Street:

The 112 space was not holy. It was a place that artists could call their own—a real alternative. Each artist set up hours, actually moved in, and worked in a really free way. [George] Trakas cut a hole in the floor. It was a completely different way of making sculpture. You didn't even think about it, you just responded to the place.[4]

Site-specific installations flourished at 112 Greene Street, which was founded by the artist Jeffrey Lew in 1970. Formerly a rag-salvaging business, the old industrial space included a ground floor and a basement level. Lew's policy was to show unknown and well-known artists together. Many of the works created at 112 Greene Street were characterized by their reciprocal relationship to the space itself. The works shown were often executed on site, with the artists incorporating the rough, unfinished floors and walls.

112 Greene Street was also a site for performance, occasionally using installations as sets. There was an exchange between artists, dancers, and filmmakers. Suzanne Harris built several pieces of moving sculpture that could be improvised on by dancers. In March 1973, she installed several pieces of sculpture including *The Wheels,* a giant set of gears that could be moved via pressure on bars attached to the cogs. In that same exhibition was a piece she constructed called *Flying Machine,* which was a harness that could hold and suspend a dancer. Tina Girouard's performance, *Live House,* involved the performers designating different parts of the 112 Greene Street space as different rooms in a house. Each performer portrayed a different room, using a variety of materials. After the performance, the materials used remained on view.

In the first several years of 112 Greene Street's existence, Gordon Matta-Clark was a pivotal figure there. This was due to a combination of the work he did and his ability to draw a community of people around him. One of his first works at 112 Greene Street consisted of a hole he dug in the basement that he wanted to be deep enough to expose the foundation of the building. Eventually he planted a tree in this hole, which survived under infrared lights for three months. In *Open House,* 1972 (also known as *Drag on* or *Dumpster*), Matta-Clark installed partitions and doors in an old industrial container outside 112 Greene Street, which became the site for numerous performances. People activated the space by walking through it or actually performing in it. But most of Matta-Clark's environmental works were not done on site at 112 Greene Street or at any other alternative spaces. His unique form of Installation art, which involved cutting away parts of buildings, began with his own living space, and soon moved on to abandoned buildings around New York. He showed fragmented relics from the buildings at 112 Greene Street and did other projects there, but he increasingly worked away from even the margin of the art world. This was part of a conscious program, as reflected in his 1977 statement:

The whole question of gallery space and the exhibition convention is a profound dilemma for me. I don't like the way most art needs to be looked at in galleries any more than the way empty halls make people look or high rise city plazas create life-less environments. And even though my work has always stressed an involvement with spaces outside the studio-gallery context, I have put objects and documentation on display in gallery spaces All too often there is a price to pay due to exhibition conditions: my kind of work pays more than most just because the installation materials end up making a confusing reference to what was not there. But for me, what was outside the display became more and more the essential experience.[5]

The relationship between objects exhibited in a gallery and a larger site from which they were taken had begun to be explored by Robert Smithson at the end of the 1960s. Smithson used the terms "sites" and "nonsites," to describe the transfer of material from a site outside the museum or gallery to an indoor space. For Matta-Clark, both the site and nonsite were part of the urban environment.[6]

In a purist sense, Matta-Clark was what might be called an Installation artist's artist. There is arguably no installation less portable, none more ephemeral and site specific nor more opposed to the art market, than his cutaways in buildings slated for demolition in the New York area and environs. His cutaways proved even more ephemeral than most Earthworks, which, although nature might take its toll on them, are not usually slated for complete and immediate destruction. Also, unlike remotely situated Earth art, Matta-Clark's work was within a social context, rather than removed from society. He created his works within existing architecture—spaces created by humans for humans, and his work both altered and called attention to these spaces. He expressed his intentions in this regard:

I have chosen not isolation from the social conditions, but to deal directly with social conditions, whether by physical implication, as in most of my building works, or through more direct community involvement, which is how I want to see the work develop in the future. I think that differences in context is my primary concern—and a major separation from Earth art. In fact, it is the attention paid to specific, occupied areas of the community.[7]

Matta-Clark did not introduce new materials into the space of these cutaways; instead he removed some of what was there. Whether or not spectators visited his works, the spectator's presence was implied, because Matta-Clark most often worked with residential architecture. The spaces could be entered and walked around before the building came down. It is easy to imagine how jarring the experience of standing in *Splitting: Four Corners,* 1974, a single-family house that he had cut nearly in half, would have been (figure 4.2). This unsettling effect is confirmed by eyewitness accounts. Peter Schjeldahl wrote of the cutaways: "Matta-Clark's chain-sawed environments make meaning by intensifying physical self-consciousness to ecstatic or terrifying effect. They are symbols of a life in art conducted outside the upholstered prisons of commerce and institutions, an uncontained existence requiring moment-to-moment location checks: Where am I? Furthermore: What am I and what am I doing?"[8] Schjeldahl's last words sum up a basic response to being in an installation that is expressed in varying forms beginning with the critical response to the Environments of Kaprow, Oldenburg, and Dine, and continuing on from there.

There was an implicit social agenda to Matta-Clark's work which eventually became more explicit. In a 1977 interview, Matta-Clark discussed the social issues generated by his work:

By undoing a building there are many aspects of the social conditions against which I am gesturing: first to open a state of enclosure which had been pre-

conditioned not only by physical necessity but by the industry that profligates suburban and urban boxes as a context for insuring a passive, isolated consumer—a virtually captive audience. The fact that some of the buildings I have dealt with are in Black ghettos reinforces some of this thinking, although I would not make a total distinction between the imprisonment of the poor and the remarkably subtle self-containerization of higher socioeconomic neighborhoods.[9]

Toward the end of his abbreviated life, Matta-Clark was getting involved with the community on New York's Lower East Side.[10] He conceived of a plan to create a resource center and youth program that would salvage buildings and materials from the neighborhood. At the same time, his works became increasingly involved with museums, or, as Brian Hatton put it, "aimed at museums."[11] *Circus (Caribbean Orange)* was commissioned by the Museum of Contemporary Art in Chicago in 1978. It was a cutaway piece done in a townhouse that was going to be incorporated into the museum. It was handled with full museum attention, complete with tours for visitors and museum guards, but the piece was demolished when renovation of the townhouse began. The museum later referred to this work as an "extallation."[12] One of Matta-Clark's last projects proposed a cutaway of the facade of the Museum of Modern Art. The facade, although not slated for demolition, was slated for removal in conjunction with the museum's expansion.

George Trakas is another artist associated with the early years at 112 Greene Street who created installations that incorporated the space and the spectator. Trakas has done indoor and outdoor pieces, as well as ones that span both. ↑↓ *(The Piece That Went Through the*

Floor) and ⇆ (The Piece That Went Through the Window) were two important works done by the artist at 112 Greene Street in 1970. His ⇆ had components that began indoors and continued out the window (see figure I.5). The piece consisted of a large sheet of glass that was supported by a wood and wire structure. A pile of sawdust was heaped up on one side of the glass. The whole structure was held up by a taut rope that went out of the window of the building and was fastened to the opposite wall of the airshaft, allowing the piece to relate to the world outside of the exhibition space. After only a few days, ⇆ (The Piece That Went Through the Window) collapsed when a heavy rain relaxed the tension on the rope, an outcome the artist had anticipated—the piece was not meant to last. ↑↓ (The Piece That Went Through the Floor) spanned two floors of 112 Greene Street. A hole cut in the floor allowed both floors to be seen simultaneously, exposing more information about the building than was originally available, as well as providing a certain amount of bodily risk for the viewer. Cutting the hole and leaving it for the viewer also drew attention to the nonrarefied character of the space: it was possible to make a big hole in it. The following year, in 1971, Trakas had two works included in the Guggenheim exhibition *Ten Young Artists: The Theodoron Awards.* Not surprisingly, Trakas did not cut any holes into the Guggenheim Museum floor, or into any other part of the museum. Nor did either of the pieces, *Locomotive* and *Shack,* have components that continued outdoors. They were self-contained pieces that could be shown in other spaces. 112 Greene Street allowed the artist freedoms that were impossible to replicate in a museum context.

↑↓ (The Piece That Went Through the Floor) and ⇆ (The Piece That Went Through the Window) were both scaled to human proportions.

Hugh Davies has said of Trakas that "[his] body-scaled, handcrafted structures are stage sets or playgrounds which are incomplete without the spectators' presence, indeed their active participation."[13]

It is worth noting that Trakas was involved with the Judson dance scene in the late 1960s. His interest in choreography carried over to his installation work, in which the movements and possibilities for the positioning of the spectator are given careful consideration. But his background in dance was only one factor, as Trakas himself has stated: "In looking at a lot of work in the sixties, I found myself disturbed by the fact that I could arbitrarily start looking at a work from any point of view. In my work I wanted to confront the spectators directly and draw them in physically to discover space with their bodies."[14] 112 Greene Street was a place where this could happen.

4.3
Michael Asher, *Clocktower*, 1976. Installation view of thirteenth floor exhibition area. Viewing north. New York. 30 March through 15 April, 1976. Photograph by Helen Winkler.

4.4
Michael Asher,
Clocktower, 1976.
Detail of architec-
tural ornament of
the fourteenth floor
porch. New York.
30 March through
15 April, 1976.
Photograph by
Daniel Buren.

One of the most dramatic site-specific installations at an alternative space in New York in the 1970s was done by Michael Asher at the Clocktower in 1976. Asher had participated in both the *Spaces* exhibition and the Whitney's *Anti-Illusion: Procedures / Materials* exhibition. In *Spaces,* Asher had responded to the sealed-off quality of the institution by creating a pristine room that absorbed sound. His installation at the Clocktower responded to the freer spirit of the place. Directed by Alanna Heiss, the Clocktower provided three floors of exhibition space at the top of a building at 108 Leonard Street in lower Manhattan. Asher whitewashed the somewhat decrepit walls, and removed all exterior doors, windows, and related fixtures of the three-story space (figure 4.3). In contrast to his work in *Spaces,* street sounds, smells, weather conditions, and any flying debris were all invited into the emptied building for the three-week run of the exhibition. For the viewer, Asher had created a situation where being in the building was the same as being in the piece; there was absolutely no separation between the two. He would later recall:

The intention was to enable viewers, once having entered the interior of the installation, to find the exterior to be as important as the interior. . . . I wanted to merge interior and exterior conditions, that is, exterior noise, air, light, and pollutants with the conditions existing in the interior.[15]

One reviewer described how "the whole exhibition space seemed to breathe like city folk visiting the mountains for the first time—inhaling ecstatically and exhaling reluctantly."[16] It was a piece that could not have been done anywhere but an alternative space. As Nancy Foote commented in her review of the work: "Asher is admitting the things that the conventional gallery takes pains to seal off. The outside, with all its real-life pollution, comes pouring in—Pandora's box reversed. Somehow this invasion poses little threat to the Clocktower, which has never made any claims to pristine isolation."[17] Asher hoped to alter the traditional way of viewing sculpture "since the outside was objectified and integrated through the once hermetically sealed doors and windows"[18] (figure 4.4).

Patrick Ireland showed his first installation at 112 Greene Street in 1973. As an art critic writing for publications including the *New York Times* in the early 1960s, Brian O'Doherty, as Ireland was still known then, had seen and experienced firsthand the Environments of Kaprow, Dine, Oldenburg, and their contemporaries. Later, in 1969, he became the director of the Visual Arts Program at the National Endowment for the Arts, succeeding Henry Geldzahler. In this capacity, he supported the growth of alternative exhibition spaces and the work shown in them. He encouraged Jeffrey Lew to apply for NEA grant money for 112 Greene Street, and it was in part because the Endowment required certain documentation that 112 Greene Street began to keep more detailed records of its exhibition program. In addition to his other roles, O'Doherty was the editor of *Art in America* from 1971 to early 1974. Because of his dual roles as artist and critic, his perspective has a particular authority. On Installation art he has said: "My criterion for an installation was what do you do with the space. . . ? What cues did you take from it? How did you manipulate, alter, reconfigure, redesign it for another category or variety of experience?"[19] His own work is guided by these questions. The emphasis on space is ultimately geared toward creating the opportunity for an experience for the viewer.

Ireland installed *Rope Drawing #1* at 112 Greene Street in 1973. The piece consisted of a floor-to-ceiling grid made of rope, which divided the space of 112 Greene Street into two sections. Another rope drawing, at the Betty Parsons Gallery a year later, consisted of strings looped loosely from one side of a wall to the other, above the viewers' heads. He not only worked with the space, anchoring the ropes directly onto the wall, but created an environment of sorts in which the individual could control his or her perception of the piece. The experience of seeing this work was described by a reviewer as follows:

In the anteroom of the gallery a rope sculpture, resembling the ribcage of a dinosaur, almost engulfs the space and creates an environment. . . . The various angles from which the ribs are viewed fascinate the beholder, mixing shadows on the walls with crossing lines of the physical piece. Consequently this aesthetic sculpture engages the viewer in a perceptual dialogue.[20]

Ireland placed, and continues to place, a great deal of emphasis on the viewer as participant. He has expressed the importance of this issue: "[My] work . . . has a . . . conception of the viewer, not as an eye, nor a brain, nor a bundle of reflexes moving a corpus around, but one that offers a person to make his own space, to live in his own space."[21]

The ability of Ireland's work to elicit this sort of response from the viewer was borne out even when the work was in a museum context, rather than an alternative space. Regarding *One Drawing in Two Rooms,* a rope drawing installation he did at the Los Angeles County Museum of Art in 1975, Ireland reported that "months later, the work was still there but with additions. Kids with books, kids without books, some with happy unfocused eyes, adults, came in and hung out—sitting around the walls, talking, reading, doing nothing. The space had become a place."[22]

In his more recent work, Ireland has become involved with establishing sight lines by providing a fixed point on which the viewer can stand. From this vantage point, his works, which now involve painted walls as well as his signature rope, allow the viewer to line up the elements to create a sense of perspective. In 1998 at the Charles Cowles Gallery in SoHo, Ireland created *Entrance to the Garden of Earthly Delights* (figure 4.5). From a dot on the floor in the center

4.5
Patrick Ireland, *Entrance to the Garden of Earthly Delights*, 1998. Charles Cowles Gallery. Rope, latex paint. Courtesy Charles Cowles Gallery, New York.

of the space, the viewer could slowly rotate, looking at all four sides of the space, and visually align the taut strings with the abstract architectural forms on the walls. Suddenly the web of ropes falls into place, and an illusion of deep space is created. The viewer is still free to move all around the space, but the logic of the piece is only accessible from one point, which will vary depending on the height of the individual viewer.

Ireland, Matta-Clark, and Mary Miss were among the seventy-eight artists who participated in the inaugural exhibition for P. S. 1 in Long Island City, an alternative space opened in 1976 by Alanna Heiss. The exhibition was called *Rooms (P.S. 1)*. In Heiss's brief statement in the catalog, she wrote:

Rooms (P.S. 1) represents an attempt to deal with a problem. Most museums and galleries are designed to show masterpieces; objects made and planned elsewhere for exhibition in relatively neutral spaces. But many artists today do not make self-contained masterpieces; do not want to and do not try to. Nor, are they for the most part interested in neutral spaces. Rather, their work includes the space it's in; embraces it, uses it. Viewing space becomes not frame but material. And that makes it hard to exhibit. . . .

Art changes. The ways of exhibiting must change too.[23]

The guiding principle of the exhibition was site specificity, and the artists addressed this. Many created room-size works that the viewer could enter. These works were not necessarily constructed at the site. Mary Miss presented *Sapping,* 1975, a work that was portable. Constructed from plywood, with steel flooring, it was a narrow corridor that could be entered and traversed. The floor of the piece had

4.6
Mary Miss,
Sapping, 1975.
Wood, paint, steel.
72 x 36 x 240
inches. Collection
of the artist.

several levels, each one rising progressively higher, and pressing the viewer closer to the ceiling (figure 4.6). Barbara Baracks described the experience of *Sapping:* "One of her baldest satires on optic laws is *Sapping,* 1975—a plywood corridor each of whose three succeeding sections is abruptly narrower and higher. It's harder to saunter into that corridor than into your average cul-de-sac, and once inside the optics invite the intruder to step (hastily) outside."[24] Howardena Pindell also described *Sapping:* "One feels, walking around and into *Sapping,* as if one has been edged into a symbolic dimension as Gulliver or a Lilliputian. *Sapping*—a nonpictorial installation—has subliminal references to high walls, fences, steps, water (dull alu-

4.7
Suzanne Harris, *Peace for the Temporal Highway,* 1976. Installation view, *Rooms (P. S. 1).* P. S. 1 Contemporary Art Center, New York. 9 June through 26 June 1976. Photograph by Suzanne Harris. Courtesy of the estate of Suzanne Harris.

minum flooring) and earth (raw cut wood 'walls')."[25] The sensations described by Baracks and Pindell underscore the importance of the eyewitness account for understanding this kind of work.

For the exhibition catalog, Heiss asked the participating artists to comment on either their own work or on another work in the exhibition. Several artists commented on the space and the freedom it provided. Alan Saret, who had previously done installations at 112 Greene Street, had this comment:

Let there be a new order on earth and another way of being for artists. Here at last a new kind of mark—away from the standard commercial procedure which strangles the art and artist it promises to support—far from the typical museum working with similar impact and this mark is already nicely felt, well drawn, successful. Let us create other kinds of entities to go alongside this one to make contrast and variety for a new order.

Saret's contribution to the exhibition was *The Hole at P.S. 1, Fifth Solar Chthonic Wall Temple*. The piece consisted of a hole that the artist had put into a wall, exposing the brick behind the plaster.

Suzanne Harris created a work for *Rooms* entitled *Peace for the Temporal Highway* (figure 4.7). Described in the catalog as the truncation of one-half a cube, it was a shaped room with a twenty-five-degree- and a forty-five-degree-angle wood frame on which cardboard was nailed. This work elicited interesting comments from other artists in the exhibition—comments that vividly evoked the experience of the piece. Sue Weil described it as "The experience of feeling tiny or of no size in a field or on a beach—The experience of feeling as if you suddenly grow large as you step into a phone booth—

SUZANNE HARRIS' room is that focused Lewis Carroll experience." In the comments about Harris's piece, the first-person point of view was used to describe the experience of being there. Jene Highstein said, "There's the room and then you're in a flat sided tapering but light tunnel going down to a square door you bend down and walk through. Fast even if you walk slowly. Inside the room, the form comes down to the door making a 3-d wedge into the room. Your eye mostly up and then away towards the ceiling, you remember the entry standing with the cardboard form."

There were some comments in the catalog on the lateness of P.S. 1 as an enterprise (most of the alternative spaces had opened a few critical years earlier), and of the difference between the 1960s and the 1970s. Douglas Davis remarked:

P.S. 1 was of course an important *occasion*. It had a sense of the past about it as well as the present. The party, the band, the dancing had a 60's feeling and thus cheered up those who miss all of that in the current time. Most of the work had however, another resonance. It was quieter than that, more introspective.

Vito Acconci was more skeptical, questioning the relevance of P.S. 1 in general and of the *Rooms* exhibition in particular:

Why did we all jump to be in this show? Afraid to be left out just in case "something was happening here"? Did we feel we'd better keep up a pretense of community? . . . Were we trying to find an "alternative space," or just trying to keep all the alternatives in the family? (Let's take over the alternatives before they go too far—a real alternative space, after all, would break down our defenses: with the solution—or dissolution—of distribution and marketing problems, we'd have no excuses, we'd have nothing else to do but reconsider the *kind* of work we were doing, we'd be forced to place reasons and consequences in terms of a whole world.)

Acconci implies that if an alternative space became too successful, it would no longer be able to define itself in opposition to more established spaces. This is, in fact, what has occurred to a certain extent and is symptomatic of a much larger phenomenon.

Already by the late 1970s there was a strong sense that many countercultural elements from the late 1960s and the 1970s were being recycled as mainstream commodities. The process of commercialization of "cutting edge" expression began at least as early as Woodstock and became clearly apparent in 1981 with the introduction of MTV. Quite simply, people had discovered that they could make money by packaging alternative culture.[26] The development of culture as commodity had a strong impact on the history of Installation art. Museums were beginning to look for ways to accommodate the new art, and gradually, over the next decade, Installation art would no longer be the exclusive domain of the alternative space. It would be reborn as a mainstream museum form.

After the burst of installation activity in the mid-1970s, there was a period of a few years when it seemed to die down again. Important figures including Robert Smithson, Suzanne Harris, and Gordon Matta-Clark had died early and tragically, leaving a void in their communities. Painting reemerged strongly in the 1980s, and with the "return" of painting came an art market boom. This coincided with the economic boom of the 1980s, and a widespread phenomenon during the Reagan years that is best described as the "culture of greed." The general climate of consumerism was not one in which Installation art, as it stood at the end of the 1970s, could easily flourish, although it never completely ceased.

In New York, one barometer for the new in exhibitable art is the Whitney Biennial, an exhibition that draws critical attention on the basis of what is included and what is not. During the decade of the 1980s, the Whitney consistently included Installation art as an exhibition category, along with painting, sculpture, photography, film, and video. The 1981 Biennial had a fair number of installations, including works by Jonathan Borofsky, Judy Pfaff, and Frank Gillette. Pfaff's installation, *Dragon,* surrounded the viewer with colorful plastic forms (figure 4.8). The 1983 Biennial focused on the resurgence of painting in the United States, with fewer installations, as did the 1985 Biennial. A notable installation in the latter exhibition was Dara Birnbaum's video installation, *Damnation of Faust* (figure 4.9).

Installation art in New York in the 1980s also found a sympathetic venue in the Dia Center for the Arts. First established in 1974 as the Dia Art Foundation to promote the development of the visual arts, the center "continues to place emphasis on fully developed installations of an individual artist's work over an extended period."[27] Walter De Maria's *New York Earth Room,* a long-term installation of 250 cubic yards of dirt on the floor of a pristine white room, was placed on public display by Dia in SoHo in 1980. The center opened its large Chelsea space in a renovated warehouse in 1987, providing space and support for large-scale installations.

Critics began to remark that Installation art was on the rise again in the middle of the 1980s. In a 1984 article, Dan Cameron offered a number of possible explanations for its resurgence:

4.8
Judy Pfaff, *Dragon*, 1981. Mixed media installation. Installation view of Biennial. Whitney Museum of American Art, New York. 20 January through 5 April 1981. Photograph by Geoffrey Clements.

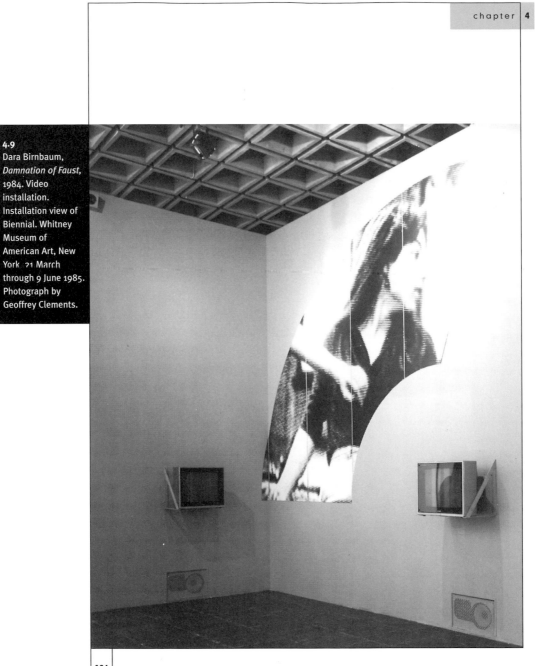

4.9
Dara Birnbaum,
Damnation of Faust,
1984. Video
installation.
Installation view of
Biennial. Whitney
Museum of
American Art, New
York, 21 March
through 9 June 1985.
Photograph by
Geoffrey Clements.

The art of installation, which seemed to be resting in semi-permanent hiber-
nation since its heyday of the mid–1970s, is back with a vengeance. Provoked
in part by a tacit acknowledgement of the increased commodity status of fine
art, and inspired at times by sincerely populist aims, these new installations are
not the random proliferations of fragments and materials that installation
came to signify a decade ago. . . . It is simply that more artists are seeing the
limitless potential of installations in terms of absolute control as opposed to
absolute abandon.[28]

The installations that form the subject of his article, by Mierle Ukeles,
Francesc Torres, TODT, and Louise Lawler/Allan McCollum, were all
done at commercial galleries. Although becoming increasingly visible,
the genre had not yet become a museum standby.

In 1988, Michael Brenson, art critic for the *New York Times,* suggested the increasing prevalence of the genre: "With the speed and
glitz of the art world, the need for the installation as a self-contained
work of art, in which visitors can be totally immersed, is not likely to
diminish."[29] As Brenson had predicted, Installation art did not diminish. In fact, by the end of the 1980s it had become widely prevalent
in the art world, and its status became that of an accepted genre that
was not only accommodated but actually sought after by major museums; Installation art was available for the commissioning. In 1992,
Holland Cotter asked:

What accounts for [Installation art's] return to popularity now? . . . Perhaps
its aura of being outside, even beyond, the milieu of the saleable object makes
it attractive to an art world whose mercantile machinery is embarrassingly
stalled. Perhaps its elastic nature and its capacity to bridge formal categories

suit an art world grown increasingly political over the past few years, where artists seek ever more dynamic ways to amplify their sociopolitical stances. Perhaps it reflects a need on the part of some artists to reclaim a metaphoric density submerged by much of the theory-based work of the past ten years.[30]

Possibly most indicative of Installation art's changing status was the selection of Jenny Holzer to represent the United States at the Venice Biennale in 1990. Holzer transformed the United States pavilion into several full-scale installations. Installation art also figured largely in the 1991–92 Carnegie International in Pittsburgh and *Documenta 9* in Kassel, Germany, in 1992.

For many reasons, exhibiting Installation art became commonplace for major art institutions by the beginning of the 1990s. The hurdles that initially made Installation art too difficult to assimilate were gradually overcome, in part because museum practice had changed somewhat, and in part because Installation art changed. By 1992, Roberta Smith observed that Installation art "is present in unprecedented quantities in museums, the very places it was supposed to render obsolete."[31] Along with institutionalization came the urge to identify formal conventions for Installation art; however, proof of this genre's continued elusiveness is found in the fact that no one identifies the same list of conventions. Nicolas de Oliveira, Nicola Oxley, and Michael Petry include just four categories in their book on Installation art: use of media technology, Earth Projects, museumification process, and responding to the history of a particular site.[32] Nancy Princenthal has also identified four conventions: theatricality, a claustrophobic sense of intimacy, the use of advanced media technologies, and obsessive composite pieces (accumulations).

Ultimately, however, she finds Installation art linked more by ideology—cultural and social critique—than by form.[33] Adam Gopnik voiced a similar thought, finding Installation art "unified more by a common ideology than by a common set of forms—unified more by what it is trying to accomplish than by the way it looks." According to Gopnik, artists are trying through Installation art "to score topical points and raise consciousness about particular issues."[34] The ideology mentioned by both Gopnik and Princenthal is a reference to the widespread inclusion of political subject matter in Installation art.

Roberta Smith also has identified a number of formal conventions. Her list of what she refers to as the clichés of contemporary Installation art include "Delusions of High Tech," in which "a lot of artists are spending too much time with sophisticated equipment in darkened rooms,"; "The Shock of the Real," in which "Installation art can imitate life to unusual degrees, often by simply commandeering it"; "The Shock of the Old," in which "eroded materials and objects redolent of natural decay or human use" are overemphasized; "Going for the Jugular," in which "inherently heart-rending topics" are sensationalized in three-dimensional space; and "When More Is Just More," referring to works which display a large accumulation of just one thing.[35]

Institutionalization has had a significant effect on Installation art. Not surprisingly, once installations became the domain of mainstream museums, they lost some of their cutting-edge character. This did not deter artists from wanting to show their installations in museums. Installation art is a showcase form that needs a public space in order to exist, and museums are the most validating of public spaces. As Ilya Kabakov said, "The alternative spaces (Documenta) are not the highest level of art . . . as museums are, and placement of installations into museum sacred space makes installation also sacred." [36]

The Museum of Modern Art is one such sacred space. In 1991, the institution offered seven artists the opportunity to create installations. The resulting exhibition, *Dislocations,* was the first group exhibition of Installation art at the Museum of Modern Art since the *Spaces* exhibition in 1969. Between 1969 and 1991 there were Projects that could be described as Environments or installations, but no full-scale exhibitions of Installation art such as this one. *Dislocations* not only took over an entire floor of the museum's temporary exhibition space as well as the area normally reserved for contemporary art from the permanent collection, but it even invaded the space dedicated to the permanent collection of European art on the second floor. *Dislocations* was the first exhibition curated for the Museum of Modern Art by Robert Storr. It consisted of installations by Louise Bourgeois, Chris Burden, Sophie Calle, David Hammons, Ilya Kabakov, Bruce Nauman, and Adrian Piper. The mix of gender, race, and nationality may have been a response to the criticism that was still aimed at the museum.

The Nauman piece, entitled *Anthro/Socio,* consisted of a large, darkened room with giant video screens and monitors against the walls (figure 4.10). On the screens loomed close-up images of the head of a man who was incessantly mouthing the words "feed me/eat me/help me/hurt me/anthropology/sociology." The heads were alarmingly large and bald. Accompanying recordings of the words, mixed to sound almost like Gregorian chants, reverberated throughout the room. The sounds did not correspond to the lip movements of the heads, creating a disjunctive experience.

Leaving the Nauman room to head toward Kabakov's installation, the viewer entered a narrow passageway that led to an even narrower bridge. From this delicate perch, Kabakov provided the viewer
with a scene that was intended to represent the destruction of a community center. Dozens of tiny white figures were strewn all over the
floor, along with overturned furniture and paintings leaning against
the walls. The figures could be viewed with the naked eye, but
Kabakov had also provided a single pair of binoculars that was fixed
to the bridge. There was a text panel on the bridge describing the fic-
tional events that had led to this scene of destruction. There was a natural crowd control element in the narrowness of the bridge and the
placement of the text panel and binoculars.

4.10
Bruce Nauman,
Anthro/Socio, 1991.
Video installation.
Installation view of
the exhibition
Dislocations. The
Museum of Modern
Art, New York. 16
October 1991
through 7 January
1992. Photograph ©
1999 The Museum
of Modern Art,
New York.

After leaving this space, there was a room containing Bourgeois's *Twosome,* which consisted of two enormous horizontally oriented oil drums that fit one inside the other. The cylinders were set up so that one moved in and out of the other in a slow mechanical motion, with glowing red light emanating from them. Viewers were not moved to touch the work, as there was a sense that they could easily catch their fingers in the movement.

Upstairs on the third floor, Adrian Piper had constructed *What It's Like, What It Is, #3,* a bright white, terraced arena topped with a narrow band of mirror. The work addressed the pain of racist stereotyping. In the center of the room was a four-sided video monitor on which an African American man slowly, and with great dignity, repeated phrases including "I'm not stupid. . . . I'm not lazy."

4.11
Adrian Piper, *What It's Like, What It Is, #3,* 1991. Installation view of the exhibition *Dislocations.* The Museum of Modern Art, New York. 16 October 1991 through 7 January 1992. Photograph © 1999 The Museum of Modern Art, New York.

Spectators could sit on one of the shiny white ledges and see themselves reflected in the mirror, while watching the face in the video (figure 4.11).

Next door to the Piper piece was Chris Burden's *The Other Vietnam Memorial,* a gigantic copper book standing upright and open all around like a Rolodex. The heavy pages, which could be slowly turned by the viewer, were etched with three million computer-generated names representing the Vietnamese people killed during the Vietnam War. The piece was meant to serve as the other side of the story told by Maya Lin's Vietnam Memorial in Washington, D.C.

The last installation on the third floor was David Hammons's *Public Enemy* (figure 4.12). The room was cluttered with various elements; the artist had covered every surface except the floor-to-

4.12
David Hammons.
Public Enemy, 1991.
Mixed media
installation.
Installation view of
the exhibition
Dislocations.
Museum of Modern
Art, New York. 16
October 1991
through 7 January
1992. Photograph
© 1999 The Museum
of Modern Art,
New York.

ceiling window that is a permanent part of the gallery space. Balloons hung from the ceiling, real autumn leaves crunched underfoot, and elegant wallpaper lined the walls. The sound of a helicopter reverberated overhead. The room contained a giant photo blowup of the statue of Theodore Roosevelt on horseback, flanked by Native American and African figures, which stands in front of the American Museum of Natural History. The photo blowup was surrounded by sandbags on which were mounted guns and sticks of dynamite that were aimed at the image. Police barricades held the viewer back from the whole arrangement.

Sophie Calle's piece, *Ghosts*, involved removing five works from the permanent collection and replacing them with comments made about them elicited by the artist from various museum personnel. The texts of these comments were screened onto the wall in the same dimensions as the missing paintings.

The effect on the third floor was of three completely separate exhibitions, because the rooms were laid out along a corridor and did not function as passageways from one to the next. Downstairs, where the Nauman, Kabakov, and Bourgeois pieces were installed, this autonomy was more difficult to achieve, particularly because sound from the Nauman installation penetrated the other two. The museum created dark passageways between the three works, and although this helped each to maintain its own atmosphere, it also obliterated any sense of the structure of the museum space.

Some of the reasons why the museum gave Storr the go-ahead to do an exhibition of Installation art might be gleaned from the materials generated for public consumption. The press release for *Dislocations* noted that the works "have been created especially for this exhibition."[37] This is one of the reasons museums show Installation art: to demonstrate that there is an active relationship between the institution and the art community. If an artist has made a work especially for the museum, cooperation between the two parties is implied. The catalog for *Dislocations* included photographs of each of the artists at work installing his or her piece in the museum, reinforcing the connection between the artists and the museum. Presumably, that connection speaks to the continued relevance of the museum overall. Installation art also creates, in theory, a closer connection to the viewer. As critic and curator Benjamin Weil notes, with Installation art, "the development of the artist's body of work is revealed to the viewer in its totality, from the conception of the project to its realization; the result is a much closer relationship between artist and audience."[38] This relationship is also desirable from a museum's point of view, as it may make the viewer feel more privy to the creation and selection processes in the museum.

Although all the works in *Dislocations* were created especially for the exhibition, they were not all ephemeral. Both Burden's and Bourgeois's pieces, in particular, were solid, portable objects. Nonetheless, the ephemeral nature of the works was emphasized by Rona Roob, the museum archivist, in her column in *MOMA*, the members' quarterly of the Museum of Modern Art. Roob traced the history of ephemeral art at the museum beginning with *Spaces*. She then mentioned the Sol LeWitt exhibition in 1978 and the Projects series, explaining how these works were ultimately dismantled. She included Jean Tinguely's *Homage to New York,* the machine that self-destructed in the museum's garden in 1960, and emphasized the idea of works created especially for exhibition.[39]

The fact that the works in *Dislocations* were produced and shown in the context of the Museum of Modern Art affected their outcome in several ways. Art museums, in their role as patrons of Installation art, inevitably influence the outcome of the works in some way. They provide budgets for materials, allowing the potential for high technology and more polished presentations. Because of the prestige attached to showing at a major museum, commercial galleries that represent the artists are often willing to contribute additional funds. Obviously, artists are not obligated to take advantage of all that is offered. Kabakov, for example, has used refuse and throwaway materials regardless of where his installations are being presented. But the resources the museum makes available can potentially affect the direction in which an artist chooses to go. David Hammons, for one, had never before had such a large budget to work with as he did when he participated in *Dislocations.* Hammons is known for his use of discarded materials that resonate with raw human experience, such as emptied Night Train wine bottles, beer caps, chicken bones, or hair clippings. One of his early ideas for his piece in *Dislocations* had been to leave his space empty save for a slice of white bread in the middle of the room.[40] But he ultimately chose to spend his allotted funds by using materials more costly than what he normally used. Although the museum stated in a handout brochure that Hammons's "*Public Enemy* . . . transformed a white-walled Museum space, filling it with the sights, sounds and smells of the street,"[41] the piece was considered by several critics to be inconsistent with Hammons's other work. For example, Holland Cotter described it as "nowhere near as richly textured as certain other installations Hammons has done."[42] Arthur Danto found *Public Enemy* "sullen and artistically inert."[43]

Museums can undercut on several levels the effectiveness of installations done within their walls. Installations often look expensive because they are large and elaborate. Construction may be involved, or complex lighting or sound systems, so it is difficult to remain unaware that somewhere behind the installation lurks a funding source. At the same time, the artist is often pursuing a socially critical agenda that clashes with the acceptance of corporate, private, or government funds. Back in 1969, Dan Flavin had been criticized by the Art Workers' Coalition for accepting corporate funding for his piece in *Spaces*.[44] However, now that Installation art with overtly countercultural messages has blossomed in museums on a larger scale, this incongruity is brought into sharper relief.

The historical context of the museum can also have a neutralizing effect on the works. There was good reason why the alternative spaces, freed from the weight of permanent collections and thus, to a degree, from art history, had such appeal to artists making installations. Holland Cotter wrote of *Dislocations*:

One wondered how much the MOMA venue itself contributed to an absence of vitality. Had the museum's recent history of procrustean academism (all those equations! Primitivism-Modernism, Picasso-Braque, High-Low, etc.) seeped into the works? Or is it just in the nature of museums to absorb art that is potentially troublesome and reduce it to yet another meta-experience on the path between, say, Dufy on the second floor and Kiefer on the third? Not one of these installations was messy or conflicted or crazy or exquisite or hideous or transcendent—any of the things, in other words, that could have given the artists' deeply felt messages a more visceral impact.[45]

Indeed, the Museum of Modern Art's particular version of art history can have an overwhelming presence. Immortalized by Alfred Barr, especially in the famous design for the dust cover of the 1936 catalog for *Cubism and Abstract Art* (figure 4.13), the museum's version of art history has been a fairly narrow canon centered on formalist "high modernism."

Critics approached the exhibition from many different angles. The significance of the exhibition within the museum's history was remarked upon by David Deitcher: "*Dislocations* is the first serious attempt in two decades to establish MoMA's credibility as a venue for contemporary art."[46] (Here Deitcher is referring to the 1970 *Information* exhibition, not to *Spaces.*)

Some of the criticism focused on the political content of the installations. There had not been an explicit curatorial agenda in this regard—in fact the artists had been given carte blanche when creating their works—but even so, the result was an unusually political exhibition for the museum. The fact that the Museum of Modern Art was showing political art provoked a stronger critical reaction than the fact that the museum was showing Installation art. By the early 1990s, the content of much Installation art paralleled that of works in other media, being openly concerned with political and social issues. Some of the criticism launched at *Dislocations* was general criticism of contemporary political art.

For example, Adam Gopnik, in *The New Yorker,* criticized the works in *Dislocations* for appearing to have an exclusively political agenda, with no concern for aesthetics. Gopnik was not the only critic who found little aesthetic value in the works in *Dislocations:* Roberta Smith's review of the exhibition was entitled "At the

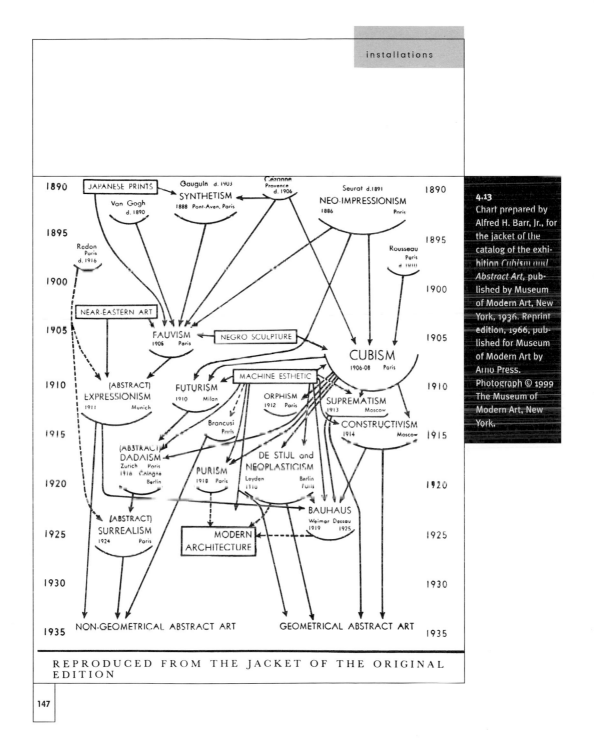

4.13
Chart prepared by
Alfred H. Barr, Jr., for
the jacket of the exhi-
bition *Cubism and
Abstract Art*, pub-
lished by Museum
of Modern Art, New
York, 1936. Reprint
edition, 1966, pub-
lished for Museum
of Modern Art by
Arno Press.
Photograph © 1999
The Museum of
Modern Art, New
York.

REPRODUCED FROM THE JACKET OF THE ORIGINAL
EDITION

Modern, Works Unafraid to Ignore Beauty." [47] Hilton Kramer, a notoriously conservative critic, found all the works in the show "equally devoid of visual appeal." He went on to say:

It is Mr. Storr's conviction, I gather, that these political tests are the only standards that are to be applied to the art of the 90's, and it is his further conviction that what is to be given priority in the art of the 90's is the ability of its creators to make us feel bad. In both respects, *Dislocations* may be said to be a rousing success. It is only as art that it fails to give us anything worth looking at. [48]

It is interesting, given Installation art's genesis, that Adam Gopnik sums it up as a form that is removed from experience and not integrated with life:

Installation art seems . . . less worldly than almost any art movement that has come before—more opaque to the uninstructed viewer, and more distant from the rhythms of lived experience. These works may claim the world, but most of them certainly don't *feel* like the world. Instead, they have a rote, self-satisfied peppiness and slickness. What one senses just beneath the contentious surface of the new installations is the complacency of the privileged. [49]

The sense of privilege Gopnik refers to stems in part from the position of the works inside the walls of the most prestigious museums. Because installations are more or less tailored to the site, the viewer is made aware of the invitational aspect of Installation art. Its relatively grandiose scale contributes to a sense of the artists being privileged in two ways: by getting special treatment from the museum (there were individual installations in *Dislocations* that were allotted more space than the entire Projects gallery) and in being somewhat above the grim "social realities" they dealt with. Indeed, the immense authority of the institution tends to diminish the socially critical stance expressed by the artist. As Danto said regarding Hammons's *Public Enemy:* "It is easy to understand the impulse to bring a vision such as [Hammons's] within the museum space, which I fear defeated it. . . . Had such a work been created in a public space, around a real monument, it might have been inspiring and even dislocative."[50]

Other comments by critics focused on the still troubling definition of Installation art as a genre. Participation and site specificity were still held up by critics as essential defining qualities, and the works were judged on the basis of how well or how poorly they incorporated them. Gopnik complains that some of the works in *Dislocations* "can be summed up in a sentence or two, and looking at them isn't very different than reading about them."[51] Holland Cotter's review also reflected on the question of what constitutes an installation. Of Burden's piece, he wrote, "The question occurs as to what made *The Other Vietnam Memorial* an installation at all. It did nothing particular with the space it occupied, nor, apart from being readable in the round, did it attempt to engage the audience physically—the very things for which the installation mode was invented."[52] Cotter's remark demonstrates how installations are still defined by ideal criteria that include site specificity and viewer participation. A work lacking in these elements is not considered an installation.

Storr uses the word *beholder,* a word associated in the vocabulary of the discourse on participation with Michael Fried, to describe what the experience can be for the viewer in *Dislocations.* Storr's opening words in the catalog, "Where are we?" establish that this kind of art can trigger this question. As Storr describes it: "Each [installation] requires the individual beholder to reconsider their identity in light of a given situation and the freedom or restriction of movement—hence perspectives—imposed upon them within it."[53] His words link the phenomenological discussions of Minimalism with work that may not be abstract. The link is the construction of a given situation that the viewer must navigate.

Dislocations had a noteworthy place within its institution's history, and the same is true of *From the Inside Out: Eight Contemporary Artists,* held at the Jewish Museum in New York in 1993. *From the Inside Out* inaugurated a new space in a renovated and expanded facility. It was one of four exhibitions that were presented when the Jewish Museum reopened its doors on June 13, 1993. The catalog of *From the Inside Out* included a chronology of contemporary art exhibitions at the museum from the time of its inception in 1947 through the 1990s, to show the long-standing commitment of the museum to contemporary art. The exhibition was curated by Susan Tumarkin Goodman, with my assistance.[54]

From the Inside Out included works by Eleanor Antin, Christian Boltanski, Clegg and Guttmann, Moshe Gershuni, Ilya Kabakov, Nancy Spero, Barbara Steinman, and Lawrence Weiner. All but the Gershuni and Steinman pieces were new works commissioned for the exhibition. The press release emphasized the participation of the artists: "*From the Inside Out: Eight Contemporary Artists,* an important exhibition of works by major international artists, will open to the public. . . . The works—many of which are being created specifically for the exhibition—address questions of personal identity, as well as those which yield answers of a broader, more universal nature."[55] No emphasis was placed in either the press release or the catalog essay by Goodman on Installation art as a genre. Installation art was mentioned only in passing, as part of a list of the genres employed by the artists. The particular characteristics of Installation art, as opposed to painting or sculpture, were not seen to require explication. There was also resistance on the part of the museum staff to play up the installation aspect of the exhibition because of the trendiness and oversaturated presence of Installation art at the time.

The floor plan of the exhibition, which had to be carefully balanced in order to satisfy everyone, was generated by the space needs of the artists. The final effect was one of crowded quarters. Some of the artists had specifically requested spaces that would be more isolated, but in the end, with the exception of the Kabakov piece, each room was also a passageway to the next work, and the self-contained quality of the installations suffered because of this. The works responded to the context of the Jewish Museum as an institution by reflecting on, criticizing, celebrating, or commenting on Jewishness in some way.

Eleanor Antin created *Vilna Nights*, a tableau of a ruined Jewish ghetto that incorporated film. The piece was constructed in California, shipped to New York, and reconstructed. Boltanski made *Museum of the Bar Mitzvah,* an installation including display cases filled with objects related to the American bar mitzvah (figure 4.14). Clegg and Guttmann created a photographic reconstruction of a section of the library of the Jewish Theological Seminary—the museum's parent organization. Moshe Gershuni contributed paintings and sculpture with Hebrew lettering and phrases. Kabakov created an installation entitled *Mother and Son* that focused on his mother's life in Russia (see figure I.1). Nancy Spero screened text directly onto the wall that related to aspects of Jewish women in history. Barbara Steinman included *Signs,* a work composed of sixty light boxes arranged around the perimeter of the room, flashing the word *Silence,* and another piece called *Of a Place Solitary. Of a Sound Mute,* which was concerned with concentration camp victims. Lawrence Weiner painted Hebrew and English words into a corner of the gallery, using the metaphor of substances that explode when combined to address the anachronism of Jewish dietary laws.

Different types of experiences were offered to the viewer in the different works. The Kabakov piece, *Mother and Son,* allowed the

4.14
Christian Boltanski, *Museum of the Bar Mitzvah*, 1993. Mixed media installation. Installation view of *From the Inside Out: Eight Contemporary Artists*. Jewish Museum, New York. 13 June 1993 through 14 January 1994. Photograph © Patricia Layman Bazelon. Courtesy of Marian Goodman Gallery, New York.

viewer to enter the room and be surrounded by the environment that Kabakov had created. To some extent, the experience was tightly controlled by the artist. Only six people were allowed in the room at one time, and to ensure this, a guard was hired to stand near the entrance of the space. The room was almost completely dark; the only light source was a painted-over lightbulb hanging from the ceiling. Visitors were required to use a flashlight when entering the space, but only six flashlights were provided, so people had to wait for someone to come out before they could get a flashlight and go in. Once inside, the viewer had to duck under the strings of refuse and Russian and English texts strung across the room. The flashlight could be used to illuminate works on the walls as well, at the viewer's own discretion. In that respect, the viewer controlled his or her own perception of the piece.

From the Inside Out was discussed by critics within the context of the reopening of the museum. The museum was somewhat successful in its mission to redefine itself through the exhibition. Kay Larson, writing for *New York* magazine, said:

In the sixties, the Jewish Museum put on some legendarily important exhibitions including "Primary Structures," the first public identification of Minimalism. In the seventies it turned its attention back to religion. Now the museum seems to be signaling an interest once again in the great American landscape where artists live and work. . . .

Now that the Jewish Museum has 4,000 years of history on view upstairs, perhaps it feels freer to expand its mission again.[56]

The lateness of doing an exhibition of Installation art was brought up by Roberta Smith: "The less said about 'Inside Out' the better.

Installed on the museum's ground floor, it is a cramped and well-behaved show of installation art that mostly points out the academization, or domestication, of the genre."[57]

Dislocations and *From the Inside Out* demonstrate an important aspect of showing installations at museums that is not visible to the viewing public: the collaborative relationship between the artist and the curator, a relationship that sometimes redefines the role of the latter. The genesis of the Boltanski piece in the Jewish Museum exhibition deserves particular explication in this regard.

The materials in Boltanski's *Museum of the Bar Mitzvah* were amassed by the curators, and not the artist. The conception of the piece was Boltanski's, but he left the gathering and selection of the objects, the framing of the photographs, and the construction of the display cases, up to the curators—myself included—who spent several months gathering these materials and preparing them for exhibition. The final arrangement of the photographs that hung on all four walls of the installation was left to the curators' discretion. This changed the curator's role from selecting works to direct involvement with both the content and production of the piece.

Enlisting the help of the curators did more than physically shape the piece—Boltanski's limited involvement in production allowed the museum to significantly reinterpret the project. In talking with Boltanski initially, it was clear that his conception of the American bar mitzvah was of a conspicuous display of wealth, an embarrassment of riches. The museum staff instead decided to choose more modest images, including black and white photographs of an orthodox bar mitzvah. They felt that Boltanski was overlooking the serious scholarly work that went into the bar mitzvah and so chose photographs that emphasized this aspect. Instead of including only pictures of the receptions and parties following the bar mitzvah, as Boltanski had originally instructed, the curators also chose photographs of the bar mitzvah child alone, reading texts at a podium. Boltanski wanted to include a display case of typical bar mitzvah gifts—he suggested large expensive items, such as computers. The museum staff instead selected more modest items, such as fountain pens. Boltanski voiced no objection to (indeed, did not comment on) the museum's selections, and I came away wondering if enlisting the participation of the museum had been a conscious move by the artist to see how the Jewish Museum would present the bar mitzvah. In the press release and catalog, the curatorial participation was not mentioned. Instead, these materials stated that the artist had amassed all the objects.[58] In fact, the piece may have been quite different if he had chosen the images and objects.

There are varying degrees of curatorial involvement that occur when presenting installations. By providing the initial budget and asking artists to respond to a particular site or theme, museums can potentially gain a measure of control over the works. For example, out of concern for public safety, museums can restrict viewer participation. Charlotta Kotik, curator of the Brooklyn Museum's Grand Lobby Projects, a series devoted to site-specific installation that was begun in 1984, recalls that when an artist wanted to have visitors experience his installation on the Vietnam war in a wheelchair, the museum first said no and then insisted that the chair be fixed to a track.[59] It has become commonplace for museums to have exhibitions in which the pieces are not created until the time of the exhibition, but doing so is still a leap of faith. In that respect the notion of the museum as laboratory has continued, and Installation art has changed museum process. At the same time, the ineffectiveness of many museum installations speaks to the difficulty of bringing an aesthetically and socially radical art form under institutional auspices.

Conclusion

By 1993, Installation art had reached a milestone in its short history. It had become a firmly established and flourishing genre not only in New York City, but nationally and internationally as well. As I have demonstrated, this occurred with accommodations made on all sides, by artists as well as by institutions. Installation art is now routinely exhibited and collected by major museums. Individual installations are recreated on more than one site. Exhibitions of Installation art travel from one venue to another.

Despite these changes, Installation art can and often still does offer a unique potential for viewer participation and interaction. There are numerous innovative ways that contemporary artists have exploited this aspect of the genre, providing fertile ground for future scholarship. One prominent example is Doug Aitken's prize-winning video installation, *Electric Earth,* created for the 1999 Venice Biennale. The installation included a maze of rooms through which the viewer could navigate.

Participation can include the participation of the artist. Ann Hamilton has developed a body of Installation art in which she, or occasionally another person, is present at all times, performing repetitive and absorbing tasks. For example, *Mantle,* which Hamilton created at the Miami Art Museum in Miami, Florida, in 1998, included a great pile of 60,000 cut flowers on a table. Hamilton sat on a chair in front of the table, obsessively sewing sleeves onto wool coats.

The character of Installation art in New York has continued to be formed in part by the character of the places that it occupies. The spaces where artists show Installation art are eclectic, and not always associated with the art world, margin or center. Under the auspices of the Metropolitan Transportation Authority's Arts for Transit program, Installation art can now be found at Grand Central station. Less-traveled spaces have been used by Pepón Osorio, recipient of a 1999 MacArthur Foundation "genius" award. Osorio created the installation entitled *Las Twines* in a vacant storefront in the South Bronx in 1998, and *Transboricua* in a store in East Harlem in 1999.

Within the art world, the differences between the alternative spaces and the more mainstream have at times blurred. More than twenty years have passed since P.S. 1 first opened its doors in Long Island City as a venue where artists were free to create site-specific installations. During this time, the institution continued strongly to support Installation art, among its other programs. Early in 1999, P.S. 1 and the Museum of Modern Art announced that they were merging.[60] The announcement of the merger is shocking given the history of the two institutions and P.S. 1's role in fostering radical art such as installations. This new union will undoubtedly contribute MoMA's authority to art shown at the P.S. 1 site, further establishing Installation art's legitimacy throughout the art world. The merger is tangible evidence of Installation art's evolutionary arc toward the conventional, the final move to the center.

Notes

Introduction

1. Kaprow used the word *Environment* in relation to his room-scale work at the Hansa Gallery. See Allan Kaprow, "Notes on the Creation of a Total Art" (New York: Hansa Gallery, 1958).

2. Daniel Buren, "The Function of the Studio," trans. Thomas Repensek, *October* 10 (fall 1979): 56.

3. *The Oxford Dictionary of Art,* ed. Ian Chilvers and Harold Osborne (Oxford: Oxford University Press, 1988), 253.

4. John A. Walker, *Glossary of Art, Architecture and Design Since 1945,* with a foreword by Clive Philpot, 3d ed., rev. and enl. (Boston: G. K. Hall & Co., 1992), 357.

5. Edward Lucie-Smith, *The Thames and Hudson Dictionary of Art Terms* (London: Thames & Hudson, 1984), 76.

6. Michael Fried, "Art and Objecthood," *Artforum* 5, no. 10 (June 1967): 12–23.

7. Arthur C. Danto, "Postmodern Art and Concrete Selves: The Model of the Jewish Museum," in *From the Inside Out: Eight Contemporary Artists* (New York: Jewish Museum, 1993), 21.

8. See Nicolas de Oliveira, Nicola Oxley, and Michael Petry, *Installation Art* (Washington, D.C.: Smithsonian Press, 1994); Monographs such as Maurice Berger, *Labyrinths: Robert Morris, Minimalism and the 1960s* (New York: Harper & Row Publishers, 1989); Lisa Corrin, ed., *Mining the Museum: An Installation by Fred Wilson* (Baltimore: The Contemporary, 1994).

9. André Malraux, "Museum Without Walls," in *Voices of Silence,* trans. Stuart Gilbert (Garden City, N.Y.: Doubleday & Co., 1953), 30.

10. For a discussion of Schwitters's Hannover *Merzbau,* see Dorothea Dietrich, *The Collages of Kurt Schwitters: Tradition and Innovation* (Cambridge: Cambridge University Press, 1993), 164–205.

11. Allan Kaprow, "The Legacy of Jackson Pollock," *Art News* 57, no. 6 (October 1958): 24–26, 54–55.

12. Jennifer Licht, *Spaces* (New York: Museum of Modern Art, 1969).

13. For further discussion of *Galaxies,* see Lisa Phillips, et al., *Frederick Kiesler* (New York: Whitney Museum of American Art in association with W. W. Norton, 1989), 77–78.

14. Richard Marshall, preface to *Louise Nevelson: Atmospheres and Environments* (New York: Clarkson N. Potter, 1980), 9.

15. George Dennison, "Sculpture as Environment: The New Work of Herbert Ferber," *Arts* (May–June 1963): 90.

16. See Germano Celant, "Ambient/Art," in *La Biennale di Venezia: Environment/Participation/Cultural Structures,* vol. 1 (Venice: Alfieri Edizioni D'Arte, 1976), 187–194. Celant had published a lengthy article the previous year on the subject of ambient art. See Germano Celant, "Art Spaces," *Studio International* 190, no. 977 (September–October 1975): 114–123.

17. An important exception is an exhibition space that El Lissitzky designed at the Hannover Landesmuseum in 1927–1928 for an installation of international modern art. Entitled *Abstraktes Kabinett* (Abstract Cabinet), the project was done under the direction of chief curator Alexander Dorner. For further discussion of the *Abstraktes Kabinett* see Samuel Cauman, *The Living Museum: Experiences of an Art Historian and Museum Director: Alexander Dorner,* with an introduction by Walter Gropius (New York: New York University Press, 1958), 98–108.

18. El Lissitzky quoted in Nancy J. Troy, *The De Stijl Environment* (Cambridge, Mass.: MIT Press, 1983), 126.

19. For further discussion of the *Raum für konstruktive Kunst,* see Kai-Uwe Hemken, "Pan-Europe and German Art: El Lissitzky at the 1926 Internationale Kunstausstellung," in *El Lissitzky 1890–1941: Architect, Painter, Photographer, Typographer,* ed. Jan Debbaut et al., trans. Kathie Somerwil-Ayrthon, et al. (Eindhoven: Municipal Van Abbemuseum, 1990), 46–55.

20. El Lissitzky, quoted in Sophie Küppers-Lissitzky, *El Lissitzky: Life, Letters,*

Text, trans. Helene Aldwinckle (Greenwich, Conn.: New York Graphic Society, 1967), 362.

Chapter 1

1. "Alan Kaprow's New Environment—*Words*—Experienced at Smolin Gallery," press release, 1962. Museum of Modern Art, library, New York.
2. Jim Dine, telephone interview by the author, 11 May 1995.
3. Claes Oldenburg, telephone interview by the author, 30 October 1994.
4. Claes Oldenburg, interview with Bruce Glaser, *Artforum* 4, no. 6 (February 1966): 22.
5. See, for example, Jennifer Licht, *Spaces;* Charlotta Kotik, *Working in Brooklyn: Installations* (New York: Brooklyn Museum, 1990).
6. Allan Kaprow, telephone interview by the author, 24 August 1994.
7. Joseph Ruzicka, "Jim Dine and Performance," in *Studies in Modern Art I. American Art of the 1960s,* ed. John Elderfield (New York: Museum of Modern Art, 1991), 98.
8. William C. Seitz, *The Art of Assemblage* (New York: Museum of Modern Art, 1961), 90–91.
9. Allan Kaprow, telephone interview by the author, 24 August 1994.
10. Allan Kaprow, *Assemblage, Environments and Happenings* (New York: Harry N. Abrams, 1966), 159.
11. Allan Kaprow, telephone interview by the author, 24 August 1994.
12. Allan Kaprow quoted in Michael Kirby, *Happenings* (New York: E. P. Dutton and Co., 1965), 46.
13. Allan Kaprow, telephone interview by the author, 24 August 1994. For a detailed analysis of Cage's influence on Kaprow, see Pamela A. Lehnert, "An American Happening: Allan Kaprow and a theory of process art" (Ph.D. diss., University of North Carolina at Chapel Hill, 1989).
14. Rose Moose, "Words About Kaprow," in *Words* (New York: Smolin Gallery, 1962).

15. Allan Kaprow, "About *Words*," in *Words* (New York: Smolin Gallery, 1962).

16. Ibid.

17. Andrew Ross, *No Respect: Intellectuals and Popular Culture* (New York: Routledge, 1989), 114.

18. Allan Kaprow, telephone interview by the author, 24 August 1994.

19. Ibid.

20. Allan Kaprow, telephone interview by the author, 6 March 1996.

21. For a discussion of the interrelatedness of politics and art in the downtown community at this time, see Sally Banes, *Greenwich Village 1963* (Durham and London: Duke University Press, 1993).

22. "Jumping on Tires," review of *Environments, Situations, Spaces, Newsweek,* 12 June 1961, 93.

23. Allan Kaprow, telephone interview by the author, 24 August 1994.

24. "Spring Calendar at the Judson Gallery," January–March 1960. Judson Memorial Church Archive, New York.

25. Barbara Haskell, *Blam! The Explosion of Pop, Minimalism and Performance* (New York: Whitney Museum of American Art, 1984), 26.

26. Jim Dine, telephone interview by the author, 11 May 1995.

27. Ruzicka, "Jim Dine and Performance," 102.

28. Claes Oldenburg quoted in Richard Kostelanetz, *Theater of Mixed Means* (New York: R. K. Editions, 1968), 139.

239. Claes Oldenburg quoted in Barbara Rose, *Claes Oldenburg* (New York: Museum of Modern Art, 1970), 48.

30. Jim Dine, telephone interview by the author, 11 May 1995.

31. Claes Oldenburg, telephone interview by the author, 30 October 1994.

32. Ibid.

33. Rose, *Claes Oldenburg,* 27.

34. Kurt Schwitters quoted in John Elderfield, *Kurt Schwitters* (New York: Museum of Modern Art, 1985), 12. Kirk Varnedoe also discusses Schwitters's use of throwaway materials in Kirk Varnedoe and Adam Gopnik,

High and Low: Modern Art and Popular Culture (New York: Museum of Modern Art, 1990), 63–66.

35. Jim Dine, interview by Bruce Hooten, 26 February 1965, transcript, Archives of American Art, New York.

36. Theodore Tucker, "Kaprow's 'Apple Shrine,'" *Village Voice,* 12 January 1961, 7.

37. Claes Oldenburg. Artist's statement in *Environments, Situations, Spaces* (New York: Martha Jackson Gallery, 1961).

38. Kaprow, *Assemblage, Environments and Happenings,* 182.

39. Minutes of meeting with Allan Kaprow, 2 November, 1959. Judson Memorial Church Archive, New York.

40. Ibid.

41. Allan Kaprow, telephone interview by the author, 24 August 1994.

42. Claes Oldenburg, telephone interview by the author, 30 October 1994.

43. Jim Dine, telephone interview by the author, 11 May 1995.

44. "Art: 'Up-Beats,'" *Time,* 14 March 1960, 80.

45. For a discussion of the Hansa Gallery, see Joellen Bard. *Tenth Street Days: The Co-ops of the '50s* (New York: Education, Art & Service, 1977), 8.

46. For a discussion of Richard Bellamy's career at the Hansa Gallery and the Green Gallery, see Amy Goldin, "Requiem for a Gallery," *Arts* 40, no. 3 (January 1966): 25–29.

47. Richard Bellamy, interview by Richard Brown Baker, 1963, transcript, Archives of American Art, New York.

48. For a discussion of the Reuben Gallery, see Lawrence Alloway, "The Reuben Gallery: A Chronology," in *Eleven from the Reuben Gallery* (New York: Solomon R. Guggenheim Museum, 1965).

49. For a discussion of the activities at the City Gallery and the Delancey Street Museum, see Judith E. Stein, "Red Grooms: The Early Years (1937–1960)," in *Red Grooms: A Retrospective 1956–1984* (Philadelphia: Pennsylvania Academy of the Fine Arts, 1985), 33–35.

50. Lawrence Alloway, *Eleven from the Reuben Gallery*.

51. Allan Kaprow, telephone interview by the author, 24 August 1994.

52. In 1967 Kaprow had an exhibition at the Pasadena Art Museum in which he recreated a number of his early Environments.

53. William Seitz quoted in a letter from Waldo Rasmussen to Allan Kaprow, 27 February 1963. Museum of Modern Art library, New York.

54. Allan Kaprow, telephone interview by the author, 24 August 1994.

55. Kaprow, *Assemblages, Environments and Happenings,* 316.

56. Ibid.

57. Jim Dine, telephone interview by the author, 11 May 1995.

58. Valerie Petersen, review of Allan Kaprow, *An Apple Shrine, Art News* 59, no. 9 (January 1961): 12.

59. Jill Johnston, review of Jim Dine's *Rainbow Thoughts, Art News* 59, no. 10 (February 1961): 15.

60. Petersen, review of *An Apple Shrine,* 12.

61. Theodore Tucker, "Kaprow's 'Apple Shrine,'" *Village Voice,* 12 January 1961, 7.

62. Suzanne Kiplinger, "Art: Ray-Gun," review of Ray-Gun exhibition, *Village Voice,* 17 February 1960, 11.

63. Fairfield Porter, review of Allan Kaprow's Environment at the Hansa Gallery, *Art News* 57, no. 9 (January 1959): 12.

64. Lawrence Campbell, review of Allan Kaprow's *Words, Art News* 61, no. 6 (October 1962): 13.

65. Claes Oldenburg, interview by Paul Cummings, 4 December 1973–25 January 1974, transcript, Archives of American Art, New York.

66. Jill Johnston, "'Environments' at Martha Jackson's," review of *Environments, Situations, Spaces, Village Voice,* 6 July 1961, 13.

67. Martha Jackson, interview by Paul Cummings, 23 May 1969, transcript, Archives of American Art, New York.

68. Ibid.

69. Press release for *Environments, Situations, Spaces,* 1961, Museum of Modern Art, library, New York.

70. "Jumping on Tires," 93.

71. Brian O'Doherty, "Art: 3 Displays Run Gamut of Styles," *New York Times,* 6 June 1961, 43.

72. Claes Oldenburg, interview by Paul Cummings, 4 December 1973–25 January 1974, transcript, Archives of American Art, New York.

73. Jack Kroll, review of *Environments, Situations, Spaces, Art News* 60, no. 5 (September 1961): 16.

74. Carroll Janis, telephone interview by the author, 23 June 1995.

75. Gene R. Swenson, review of *Four Environments by Four New Realists, Art News* 62, no. 10 (February 1964): 8.

76. Claes Oldenburg, telephone interview by the author, 30 October 1994.

77. Barbara Rose, "New York Letter," *Art International* 8, no. 3 (April 1964): 53.

78. John Canaday, "Hello, Goodbye, A Question About Pop Art's Staying Power," review of *Four Environments by Four New Realists* and the *First International Girlie Exhibit, New York Times,* 12 January 1964, sec. 2, 17.

79. Dore Ashton, "Four Environments, Exhibition at Janis Gallery," *Arts and Architecture* 81, no. 2 (February 1964): 9.

80. Lucas Samaras quoted in Grace Glueck, "Artifacts," review of Green Gallery exhibition, *New York Times,* 4 October 1964, sec. 2, 23.

Chapter 2

1. Richard Wollheim, "Minimal Art," *Arts Magazine* 39, no. 4 (January 1965): 26–32.

2. See Robert Storr, *Tony Smith: Architect, Painter, Sculptor* (New York: Museum of Modern Art, 1998), 27.

3. Robert Morris, "Notes on Sculpture 1," *Artforum* 4, no. 6 (February 1966): 42.

4. H. H. Arnason, *History of Modern Art,* 3d ed. (New York: Harry N. Abrams, 1986), 520.

5. Kenneth Baker, *Minimalism: An Art of Circumstance* (New York: Abbeville Press, 1988), 10.

6. John Perrault quoted in Barbara Haskell, *Donald Judd* (New York: Whitney Museum of American Art, 1988), 80.

7. Kynaston McShine, *Primary Structures: Work by Younger British and American Sculptors* (New York: Jewish Museum, 1966). For a discussion of the critical reception of this exhibition, see Bruce Altshuler, "Theory on the Floor," in *The Avant-Garde Exhibition: New Art in the 20th Century* (New York: Harry N. Abrams, 1994), 220–233.

8. Donald Judd, "Specific Objects," reprinted in Donald Judd, *Donald Judd: Complete Writing, 1959–1975* (Halifax: Press of the Nova Scotia School of Art and Design, 1975), 184.

9. Michael Benedikt, "Sculpture as Architecture," reprinted in Gregory Battcock, *Minimal Art: A Critical Anthology* (Berkeley: University of California Press, 1995), 74.

10. Robert Morris, "Notes on Sculpture II," reprinted in Gregory Battcock, ed. *Minimalism: A Critical Anthology* (Berkeley: University of California Press, 1995), 233.

11. Donald Judd, "In the Galleries," *Arts* 39, no. 5 (February 1965): 54.

12. Jacob Grosberg, "In the Galleries," *Arts* 39, no. 4 (January 1965): 54.

13. Michael Benedikt, "New York Letter," *Art International* 11, no. 1 (January 1967): 58.

14. Michael Benedikt, "Sculpture as Architecture: New York Letter, 1966–67," in *Minimalism: A Critical Anthology,* Gregory Battcock ed. (Berkeley: University of California Press, 1995), 71.

15. Michael Fried, "Art and Objecthood," *ArtForum* 5, no. 10 (June 1967): 16.

16. Barbara Haskell, *Donald Judd* (New York: Norton/Whitney Museum, 1988), 84.

17. Fried, 22.

18. Michael Fried, "Art and Objecthood," 23.

19. Michael Fried, "An Introduction to My Criticism," *Art and Objecthood: Essays and Reviews* (Chicago: University of Chicago Press, 1998), 43.

20. Ibid., 14.

21. For a summary of the origins of phenomenological readings of Minimalism, see Maurice Berger, *Labyrinths: Robert Morris, Minimalism and the 1960s* (New York: Harper & Row Publishers, 1989), 70-71, n. 41. Rosalind Krauss also discusses the origins in "Richard Serra: A Translation," reprinted in *The Originality of the Avant-Garde and Other Modernist Myths* (Cambridge: MIT Press, 1985), 262-267.

22. Krauss, "Richard Serra," 264.

23. Ibid., 267.

24. Berger, *Labyrinths,* 52.

25. Marcia Tucker, "PheNAUMANology," *Artforum* 9, no. 4 (December 1970): 38.

26. Kimberly Paice, "Catalog," *Robert Morris: The Mind/Body Problem* (New York: Solomon R. Guggenheim Museum, 1994), 94.

27. Allan Kaprow, "The Shape of the Art Environment: How Anti-Form Is Anti-Form?" *Artforum* 6, no. 10 (summer 1968): 33.

28. Baker, *Minimalism: An Art of Circumstance,* 24.

29. Ibid., 24–25.

Chapter 3

1. "Carl Andre: Artworker," interview by Jeanne Siegel, *Studio International* 180, no. 927 (November 1970): 175.

2. Carolee Schneemann, "Divisions and Rubble," in *Twelve Evenings of Manipulations,* 1967, Judson Memorial Church Archive, New York.

3. Jon Hendricks, "Some Notes, December 11, 1967," Judson Memorial Church Archive, New York.

4. Berger, *Labyrinths,* 107–114.

5. Quoted in Lucy Lippard, "The Art Workers' Coalition: Not a History," *Studio International* 180, no. 927 (November 1970): 173.

6. Lucy R. Lippard, "Notes on the Independence Movement," in *1967: At the Crossroads,* ed. Janet Kardon (Philadelphia: Institute of Contemporary Art, 1987), 23.

7. Lucy R. Lippard, "Intersections" in *Flyktpunkter/Vanishing Points,* eds. Olle Granath and Margareta Helleberg (Stockholm: Moderna Museet, 1984), 29.

8. Art Workers' Coalition, *Documents 1* (New York: Art Workers' Coalition, 1969), 114.

9. David Lee in *An Open Hearing on the Subject: What Should Be the Program of the Artworkers Regarding Museum Reform and to Establish the Program of an Open Art Workers' Coalition* by the Art Workers' Coalition (New York: Art Workers' Coalition, 1969), 39.

10. Frazer Dougherty, Hans Haacke, and Lucy Lippard, "Why MoMA Is Their Target," *New York Times,* 8 February 1970, sec. 2, 24.

11. Russell Lynes, "Conversation with Bates Lowry," *Art in America* 6, no. 5 (September–October 1968): 60.

12. See Grace Glueck, "Bates Lowry's Ouster Draws New Fire," *New York Times,* 12 May 1969, 52.

13. For a discussion of the events leading to Hightower's resignation, see Russell Lynes, *Good Old Modern: An Intimate Portrait of the Museum of Modern Art* (New York: Atheneum, 1973), 426–427.

14. For a detailed discussion of the workings of *Soundings,* see Billy Klüver with Julie Martin, "Working with Rauschenberg," in *Robert Rauschenberg: A Retrospective* (New York: Solomon R. Guggenheim Museum, 1997), 318–320.

15. Press release for *Soundings,* 22 October 1968. Museum of Modern Art, library, New York.

16. Several of the artists in *Anti-Illusion: Procedures/Materials* had also been in *9 at Castelli,* an exhibition at the Castelli Warehouse organized by Robert Morris a few months earlier.

17. James Monte, "Anti-Illusion: Procedures/Materials," in James Monte and Marcia Tucker, *Anti-Illusion: Procedures/Materials* (New York: Whitney Museum of American Art, 1969), 5.

18. Peter Schjeldahl, "New York Letter," *Art International* 13, no. 7 (September 1969): 70; and Hilton Kramer, "Art: Melting Ice, Hay, Dog Food, Etc.," *New York Times,* 24 May 1969, 31.

19. Emily Wasserman, "Process, Whitney Museum," *Artforum* 8, no. 1 (September 1969): 58.

20. Peter Schjeldahl, "Only Connect," *Village Voice,* 20–26 January 1982, 72.

21. Marcia Tucker, *Barry Le Va: Four Consecutive Installations and Drawings 1967–1978* (New York: New Museum, 1978), 46.

22. Sol LeWitt, "Paragraphs on Conceptual Art," *Artforum* 5, no. 10 (June 1967): 80.

23. Jennifer Licht to author, 17 August 1994.

24. Jennifer Licht to Walter Barciss, 23 September 1969. Museum of Modern Art, exhibition files of the Department of Painting and Sculpture, New York.

25. Jennifer Licht, *Spaces.*

26. Jennifer Licht to Larry Bell, 27 August 1969. Museum of Modern Art, exhibition files of the Department of Painting and Sculpture, New York.

27. Jennifer Licht to Franz Erhard Walther, 27 August 1969. Museum of Modern Art, exhibition files of the Department of Painting and Sculpture, New York.

28. "Audience Information of SPACES Exhibition," press release, 15 December 1969. Museum of Modern Art, library, New York.

29. Franz Erhard Walther to Jennifer Licht, 14 October 1969. Museum of Modern Art, exhibition files of the Department of Painting and Sculpture, New York.

30. For a detailed description of how Asher constructed this piece, see Michael Asher, *Michael Asher: Writings 1973–1983 on Works 1969–1979,* written in collaboration with Benjamin H. D. Buchloh (Nova Scotia: Press of the Nova Scotia College of Art and Design, 1983), 24–30.

31. Jennifer Licht to staff, 15 May 1969. Museum of Modern Art, exhibition files of the Department of Painting and Sculpture, New York.

32. Ibid.

33. "Audience Information of SPACES Exhibition," press release, 15 December 1969. Museum of Modern Art. library, New York.

34. Licht, *Spaces.*

35. Grace Glueck, "Museum Beckoning Space Explorers," review of *Spaces, New York Times,* 2 January 1970, 34.

36. Gregory Battcock, "The Politics of Space," *Arts* 44, no. 4 (February 1970): 43.

37. James Turrell to Jennifer Licht, 1969. Museum of Modern Art, exhibition files of the Department of Painting and Sculpture, New York.

38. David L. Shirey, "Art in Space," review of *Spaces, Newsweek,* 12 January,1970, 63.

39. Carter Ratcliff, "New York Letter," *Art International* 14, no. 2 (February 1970): 78.

40. Ibid., 79.

41. Robert Storr, interview by the author, tape recording, New York City, 7 October 1994.

42. Museum of Modern Art, exhibition files of the Department of Painting and Sculpture, New York.

43. Glueck, "Museum Beckoning Space Explorers," 34.

44. Jennifer Licht to author, 17 August 1994.

45. Ibid.

46. Ibid.

47. An important artist in this regard is Peter Campus. For a description of some of his important works from the 1970s, see Roberta Smith, "Peter

Campus, Bykert Gallery Uptown," *Artforum* 13, no. 8 (April, 1975): 73.

48. "Projects: Keith Sonnier," press release, 24 May 1971. Museum of Modern Art, library, New York.

49. "Projects: William T. Wiley," press release, 9 April 1976, Museum of Modern Art, library, New York.

50. Berger, *Labyrinths,* 120. "In the end, and as a result of the pressure from such organizations as the Art Workers' Coalition *and* the willingness of artists like Morris, Haacke, and Buren to exhibit in the museum, curators began to respond to the idea of reorienting the role of the exhibition."

51. Maurice Berger, "The Politics of Experience: Robert Morris, Minimalism, and the 1960s" (Ph.D. diss., City University of New York, 1988), 186.

52. Grace Glueck, "Art People," *New York Times,* 15 October 1976, sec. C., 18.

53. Berger documents this in detail in *Labyrinths,* 121–123.

54. Sir Norman Reid, "The Limits of Collecting," *Studio International* 182, no. 935 (July 1971). 38.

55. See Lawrence Alloway and John Coplans, "Talking With William Rubin: 'The Museum Concept Is Not Infinitely Expandable,'" *Artforum* 13, no. 2 (October 1974): 51–57.

Chapter 4

1. Patrick Ireland, interview by the author, tape recording, New York City, 30 January 1995.

2. Phil Patton, "Other Voices, Other Rooms: The Rise of the Alternative Art Space," *Art in America* 65, no. 4 (July–August 1977): 80.

3. Nancy Foote, "The Apotheosis of the Crummy Space," *Artforum* 15, no. 2 (October 1976): 129.

4. Alice Aycock interviewed by Joan Simon, quoted in Mary Jane Jacob, *Gordon Matta-Clark: A Retrospective* (Chicago: Museum of Contemporary Art, 1985), 33.

5. Gordon Matta-Clark interviewed by Donald Wall in Donald Wall, "Gordon Matta-Clark's Building Dissections," *Arts* 50, no. 9 (May 1976): 76.

6. Robert Pincus-Witten points out that although there are important similarities between these two artists, in practice they moved in very different circles in the art world. Pincus-Witten identifies Smithson with the "Formalist" group, and Matta-Clark with the "Informalists." See Robert Pincus-Witten, "Gordon Matta-Clark: Art in the Interrogative," in Jacob, *Gordon Matta-Clark,* 14.

7. Ibid., 77.

8. Peter Schjeldahl, "Home Wrecker: The Art of Breaking and Entering," *7 Days,* 1 June 1988, 50.

9. Gordon Matta-Clark quoted in Wall, "Gordon Matta-Clark's Building Dissections," 76.

10. Gordon Matta-Clark died of pancreatic cancer in New York in 1978, at the age of 35.

11. Brian Hatton, "Anarchitect," *Art Monthly* 169 (September 1993): 15.

12. "Art Fills Chicago Armory in 'Art at the Armory: Occupied Territory,'" press release, fall 1992, Museum of Contemporary Art Chicago, 2.

13. Hugh M. Davies, "George Trakas," in Hugh M. Davies and Sally E. Yard, *George Trakas Log Mass: Mass Culture* (Amherst: University Gallery, University of Massachusetts, 1980), 1.

14. George Trakas interviewed by Hugh M. Davies and Sally E. Yard in Davies and Yard, *George Trakas Log Mass,* 55.

15. Michael Asher, *Michael Asher: Writings 1973–1983 on Works 1969–1979,* 126.

16. Peter Frank, "Michael Asher," *Art News* 75, no. 7 (September 1976): 123.

17. Nancy Foote, "Michael Asher, The Clocktower," *Artforum* 14, no. 10 (June 1976): 64.

18. Michael Asher, *Michael Asher: Writings 1973–1983 on Works 1969–1979,* 135.

19. Patrick Ireland, interview by the author, tape recording, New York City, 30 January 1995.

20. Roberta Olson, review of Patrick Ireland's exhibition at Betty Parsons, *Arts* 48, no. 6 (January 1974): 59–60.

21. Patrick Ireland quoted in Dorothy Walker, "Patrick Ireland," in *Patrick Ireland: Purgatory* (Dublin: Trinity College, Douglas Hyde Gallery, 1985).

22. Patrick Ireland, "Sightlines," in Walker, *Patrick Ireland: Purgatory.*

23. Alanna Heiss, *Rooms (P.S. 1)* (New York: Institute for Art and Urban Resources, 1976).

24. Barbara Baracks, "Mary Miss," *Artforum* 15, no. 5 (January 1977): 58.

25. Howardena Pindell quoted in Heiss, *Rooms (P.S. 1)*, 124. The next five quotes from participating artists are drawn from the same source, 119–127.

26. For a discussion of how culture becomes mass culture, see Andrew Ross, "Containing Culture in the Cold War," in Ross, *No Respect,* 42–64.

27. "The New York Earth Room Celebrates Its Tenth Anniversary," press release, 31 January 1990, Dia Art Foundation, New York. Understanding the need for alternatives to typical museum settings, Dia also maintains long-term installations in other locations, including De Maria's *Lightning Field* near Quemado, New Mexico.

28. Dan Cameron, "Four Installations: Francesc Torres, Mierle Ukeles, Louise Lawler/Allan McCollum and TODT," *Arts* 59, no. 4 (December 1984): 66–67.

29. Michael Brenson, "A Transient Art Form With Staying Power," *New York Times,* 10 January 1988, sec. 2, 33.

30. Holland Cotter, "Dislocating the Modern," *Art in America* 80, no. 1 (January 1992): 100.

31. Roberta Smith, "In Installation Art, A Bit of the Spoiled Brat," *New York Times,* 3 January 1993, sec. 2, 31.

32. de Oliveira et al., *Installation Art.*

33. Nancy Princenthal, "Rooms With a View," *Sculpture* 9, no. 2 (March/April 1990): 26–31.

34. Adam Gopnik, "Empty Frames," *The New Yorker,* 25 November 1991, 110.

35. Smith, "In Installation Art: A Bit of the Spoiled Brat," 31.

36. Ilya Kabakov to author, June 1993.

37. "Dislocations," press release, September 1991, Museum of Modern Art, library, New York.

38. Benjamin Weil, "Remarks on Installations and Time Dimensions," *Flashart* 25, no. 162 (January–February 1992): 105.

39. Rona Roob, "From the Archives: Ephemeral Art," *MOMA* 9 (fall 1991): 23.

40. This was related by Robert Storr on a walk-through of the exhibition in October 1991, which I attended.

41. "Dislocations," handout produced by the Education Department, Museum of Modern Art. Museum of Modern Art, library, New York.

42. Cotter, "Dislocating the Modern," 104.

43. Arthur C. Danto, "Dislocationary Art," *The Nation,* 6 (January 1992): 32.

44. Glueck, "Museum Beckoning Space Explorers," 34.

45. Cotter, "Dislocating the Modern," 106.

46. David Deitcher, "Art on the Installation Plan: MoMA and the Carnegie," *Artforum* 30, no. 5 (January 1992): 80.

47. Roberta Smith, "At the Modern, Works Unafraid to Ignore Beauty," *New York Times,* 18 October 1991, sec. C, 1.

48. Hilton Kramer, "MoMA Mia, You Call This Art?," *New York Observer,* 4 November 1991, 1.

49. Gopnik, "Empty Frames," 120.

50. Danto, "Dislocationary Art," 32.

51. Gopnik, "Empty Frames," 116.

52. Cotter, "Dislocating the Modern," 103.

53. Robert Storr, *Dislocations* (New York: Museum of Modern Art, 1991), 20.

54. While assisting in the planning and execution of *From the Inside Out,* I kept a log book of discussions and proceedings. The material included here is drawn from this source.

55. "Major International Artists to Be Represented in Opening Contemporary Exhibition at The Jewish Museum," press release, May 1993, Jewish Museum, New York.

56. Kay Larson, "The Ties That Bind," *New York,* 12 July 1993, 63.

57. Roberta Smith, "Jewish Museum As Sum of Its Past," *New York Times,* 11 June 1993, sec. C, 21.

58. See Susan Tumarkin Goodman, "Eight Artists; A Cultural Context," in *From the Inside Out: Eight Contemporary Artists,* 26.

59. Charlotta Kotik, interview by the author, tape recording, Brooklyn, New York, 23 July 1994.

Conclusion

60. Carol Vogel, "A Museum Merger: The Modern Meets the Ultramodern," *New York Times,* 2 February 1999, sec. B, 6.

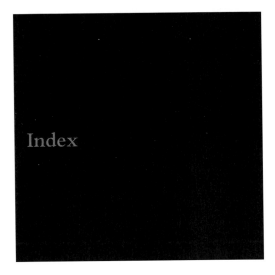

Index